School Public Relations: The Complete Book

A Source Book of Proven PR Practices

Published by the National School Public Relations Association

Table of Contents

Acknowledgment

School Public Relations: The Complete Book is written as a basic text for the development of effective and comprehensive school public relations programs for school districts and individual school buildings. It is the sequel to *Building Public Confidence For YOUR Schools,* published by the National School Public Relations Association (NSPRA) in 1978.

The book represents the very latest information in the field of school public relations gathered by NSPRA members, school superintendents and board of education members across the United States and Canada. It reflects 50 years of NSPRA's goal to advance the cause of education through responsible public relations, information and communication.

School Public Relations: The Complete Book was written by B. Rodney Davis, director-information services, Dallas (Texas) Independent School District. We deeply appreciate the contributions to the publication by the author of the previous edition, *Building Public Confidence For YOUR Schools,* J. William Jones, director of information services for the School District of Philadelphia and 1986 NSPRA president.

The book was edited by Virginia M. Ross, NSPRA director of public relations with production services by Joanna Matthews, editorial production specialist and Judi Cowan, coordinator of school communication services. John H. Wherry, ASPR, executive director of NSPRA and Rich Bagin, ASPR, director of association development, served as consultants on the book. Norma Meyer served as proof reader.

The graphics for the book were developed by Scott Photographics, Inc., and it was printed by Saul's Lithograph.

Preface

In its early years, school public relations was frequently seen as a cover-up process, as putting your best institutional foot forward, or just telling the "good news."

Today there is no longer such a naive understanding of function so basic to the successful operation of our schools. The fact is that public relations is an integral, inescapable part of school management. It is more than just news releases or speeches or slide shows, more than open house programs and newsletters, much more than just communications.

The very heart of the public relations concept as we know it today, is action in the public interest.

Today's educational public relations program is a planned and systematic management function designed to help improve the programs and services of an educational organization. It relies on a comprehensive, two-way communication process involving both internal and external publics with a goal of stimulating a better understanding of the role, objectives, accomplishments and needs of the organization. Educational public relations programs assist in interpreting public attitudes, identify and help shape policies and procedures in the public interest and carry on involvement and information activities which earn public understanding and support.

As this book was being written a public service project of the National School Public Relations Association (NSPRA) was underway. In celebration of its 50th anniversary NSPRA asked several thousand prominent citizens their opinions about the current status of education and how it could be improved. In their replies they rated schools overall as "fair" and offered critical ideas for improving them. But the key element in all replies was a recurring theme. Over and over these leading citizens stressed that a *strong educational system is vital to our democratic society*.

From this concept the nation's flag of education—the *Flag of Learning and Liberty*—was born. (See Appendix, page 223)

And, right there is the reason for this book.

Education serves a basic need in our society, but the public is often critical because it feels those needs are not being met. It is the function of school public relations:

1. To ensure that our schools are identifying and serving society's needs as well as possible, and
2. To make sure that the public knows that its needs are being met so they will support their schools.

The concept is simple. However, carrying it out requires a battery of skills and knowledge—careful planning, adequate resources and total commitment.

The National School Public Relations Association (NSPRA) exists to provide public relations help for education leaders. This book, *School Public Relations: The Complete Book*, is a sequel to the basic school PR text—*Building Confidence For YOUR Schools*—published by NSPRA in 1978. This new book includes the very latest developments in the field and approaches the subject from the same practical, "how-to-do-it," successful case studies, point of view. NSPRA's full resources are available to the reader and we invite you to call upon us at any time.

John H. Wherry, Ed.D.
Executive Director
National School Public Relations Association

CHAPTER ONE

Building Support for Your Schools

Overview

The essence, the image, the problems, the presence, even, perhaps, the mission of public education have changed dramatically in the past eight years.

When *Building Public Confidence For Your Schools* was published by the National School Public Relations Association (NSPRA) in 1978, the overview proclaimed:

"There isn't much question anymore about the status or image of public education in this country. It needs help. From the problem-plagued urban center, to the tree-lined and once trouble-free streets of suburbia, to the hills and valleys of rural America; education, particularly public education, is in serious trouble.

"It's certainly in financial trouble as the nation's tax-burdened populace rebels against education's escalating costs. And it's in trouble politically as legislators elected by the populace read the rebellion clearly and quickly join its ranks."

The overview quoted the dramatic warning of Fred M. Hechinger, the former education editor of the *New York Times*, who wrote:

"Political confusion and economic uncertainty have shaken the people's faith in education as the key to financial and social success. This retreat ought to be the most pertinent issue in any examination of the country's condition . . . At stake is nothing less than the survival of American democracy."

Yet, Hechinger noted, "none of those who are monitoring the nation's problems are paying attention to the far-reaching implications of the retreat from education. Few are aware that such a retreat is actually in progress."

In so many ways, Hechinger was right; a prophet, of sorts, ahead of his time. Yet, like so many prophets, he was shouting largely into the winds; heard only by those who wanted to hear; ignored by those, inside and outside the enterprise of American public education, who were satisfied, for a variety of reasons, including complacency, with the status quo.

Thankfully, so much has changed since then. But it did not come easy.

In 1978, the Convention Reporter of the American Association of School Administrators (AASA) quoted a speaker as saying: "We must exercise constant vigilance and political pressure and vigorous leadership if lay control of education is to survive."

In 1979, The AASA Convention Reporter stated that in "session after session . . . administrators were urged not only to renew their efforts to defend the record of public education throughout the land, but to take the initiative in an extensive public relations effort to restore public confidence in the public schools. . ."

In 1980: "The issue of public confidence was a recurring theme in nearly every session. We were told to hold our heads up high and communicate our successes." In 1981: "Public confidence in schools needs confident educators."

Sound advice. But few were listening, or, at least, believing.

Then, in the spring of 1983, came the earth tremors that literally shook the foundation of American education; the pail of cold, clear water that awakened, with a jolt, the slumbering educational enterprise; the lightning bolt that galvanized the nation's attention squarely on its public schools.

It was called *A Nation At Risk: The Imperative for Educational Reform.* It said simply, bluntly, blatantly, with about as much tact as a gauntlet across the face, that public education in the greatest nation in the world was engulfed in a "rising tide of mediocrity."

It achieved its purpose. It got our attention. Lord, did it get our attention!

Almost overnight, education vaulted to the forefront of the national agenda. State by state, community by community, citizens, educators, public officials and the media responded en masse to the report.

In June 1983, the *New York Times* said the report issued by the National Commission on Excellence in Education, "brought the issue (of education) to the forefront of political debate with an urgency not felt since the Soviet satellite shook American confidence in its public schools in 1957."

The U.S. Department of Education declared that "the ethic of excellence reasserted its strength as a beacon for American education."

The *Nation At Risk*, along with a subsequent spate of other national assessments of education, literally generated a tidal wave of reform. Initially, schools had to survive an unprecedented firestorm of critical comment and attention fueled by the report, fanned by the media, stoked by skeptical and tax-weary political entities and readily endorsed by tax-burdened communities across the nation, three-quarters of whose inhabitants had no children in the public schools.

Yet, a strange thing happened to public education on its way to Armageddon: it emerged from this frantic public and political scrutiny with its greatest public support in 20 years.

Schools, challenged, discredited, all but disenfranchised, fought back. They pledged improvement, certainly; but they also defended their record; they took the offensive; they formulated campaigns to tell their communities of their accomplishments, their plans and their visions for improvement.

Local governments, state legislatures and governors readily joined the fray. They seized the initiative. Education became a national agenda. Across the nation, the American public, after years of dissatisfaction, reaffirmed its faith in its schools, listed education high on its agenda and supported increased taxes for educational improvement.

As a result, education today is on center stage. Educational support is strong. Expectations are high. The ball is in our court.

Yet, now that we have the nation's attention, where do we go from here? Action is implied. It is demanded. But, what will it be? Confidence, to a degree, has been restored. But, how do we retain that confidence? How do we seize this unprecedented opportunity? How do we build support? Where *do* we go from here?

Historically, the pendulum always swings.

Two years of frantic acton, media attention, ultimate visibility and mandated reform have helped reposition public education in the eyes of the nation as a cornerstone upon which this country's democracy is built. The pendulum swings upward.

Yet the restoration and retention of public confidence and support of education is a continuing complex problem. Confidence, by its nature, is fragile, fleeting, fickle. It is readily influenced by the action, or inaction, of the educational enterprise at local, state and national levels. Its retention of credibility is a year-round, everyday, 24-hour endeavor.

And, education today, like society, is, or should be, in a state of awesome change.

Futurist Gloria Frazier told the NSPRA's Golden Anniversary Seminar in July 1985, at Vail, Colorado, that the employment future for our students lies in such fields as fiber optics, robotics, artificial intelligence, biogenetics, undersea mining and solar exploration.

"Just as society has shifted from an industrial to an information society," she said, "so must education make that shift to meet the needs of its students." She talked about a "strategic vision" for our rootless, nuclear, rapidly changing future; a vision that goes beyond teaching mere technical skills or even reading skills; a vision that encompasses thinking skills and coping skills and learning skills that will help today's students change tomorrow's careers many times in their adult lives.

David Pearce Snyder, another futurist at the NSPRA Seminar at Vail, looked at a future of "life-span learning" to meet the needs of "sequential careers." He talked about the need to provide students with a "set of tangible tools" so they can survive in a turbulent era of constant change that will create thousands of new jobs in their lifetimes.

Snyder looked at the schools of the future and saw them teaching students the ability to reason, to process information, to make good decisions and to keep learning.

More than at any other time in American history, he said, educators today "hold the destiny of the nation in their hands." To prepare society for a future of change, he added, "education will have to change—and change before society does—and change intelligently."

That's one hell of a mandate.

It means the continuous fine-tuning of the education process to meet both the needs of individual students and those of a progressive, drastically changing society.

Yet, the answer to retention of public confidence in education lies not only in improved educational programs, but also in a renewed commitment to developing and refining superior communication skills; skills that will enable the education industry to tell, to interpret, to market its endeavors to the publics it serves.

That is what this book is all about.

It is practical rather than theoretical. Like its predecessor, *Building Public Confidence For Your Schools*, it is a catalogue of proven public relations practices that have worked throughout the country in schools and school districts of all sizes, shapes and consistencies.

It analyzes needs and problems, guides the planning and implementation of communications, public relations and marketing activities and it provides for evaluation of results.

It will not—indeed, cannot—help a school or school district meet the complex challenges of the future in the absence of an aggressive, progressive program of education excellence. Such is education's ultimate mission, its reason for being. But it can—indeed, will—provide the education industry with clear, comprehensive, effective programs for its past accomplishments, its current endeavors and its future expectations with the ultimate judges of its success or failure, the parents and taxpayers who hold its future in their hands.

By J. William Jones, 1986 NSPRA President, director of information services for the school district of Philadelphia, and author of NSPRA's previous publication *Building Public Confidence For YOUR Schools.*

CHAPTER TWO

Public Relations

n bringing attention to the plight of the nation's schools, the National Commission on Excellence in Education, in its report, *A Nation At Risk,* did something more. It created an opportunity for improvement. Schools survived an unprecedented firestorm of critical comment and attention from the press to emerge with greater public support than at any time in the recent past.

Education on Public Agenda

In a letter to NSPRA members after the report was issued, John H. Wherry, executive director of the National School Public Relations Association, called on school public relations practitioners to "seize this opportunity." Wherry wrote:

"Education is clearly now on the public's agenda, and I believe we have the best opportunity we have ever had to keep it there, to focus the public's attention on our problems and our accomplishments and to make education the high public priority it must be if we are to achieve excellence. We have an obligation to act now. We must promote dialogue, discussion and then action to achieve excellence."

In other words, it's time that educators and boards of education stopped being embarrassed about mounting an effective public relations campaign and went on the offensive to tell their story clearly and compellingly to the public, the press, the politicians and anyone else who will be responsible for helping improve the image of education in the months and years ahead.

An Act of Social Responsibility

Edward L. Bernays, author of the 1923 book *Crystalizing Public Opinion,* counselor to presidents, corporations and government agencies for the past 60 years, and generally regarded as the father of public relations in the United States, calls the task of salvaging education through better public relations "possibly the most important in the country, because the future of the country depends on it."

Bernays contends that school systems must not be frightened off by the "semantic tyranny" of those who would oppose the concept of public relations in education, because true public relations is an act of "social responsibility."

"In America," he says, "words are as fragile as lace or a soap bubble. The words and their meanings get kicked around . . . so today the words 'public relations' are so muddy in meaning that to some they do mean press agentry or flackery."

The Most Important Task We Face

"Building and maintaining public confidence in education is the most important single task we face. And the effort demands that educators develop sophisticated understanding of the public relations process.

"Education can no longer afford the naive view that public relations is only publicity through newspapers, radio and TV; that PR is telling people just those things that make schools look good; that PR is just a cosmetic approach to dealing with our problems. Unfortunately, many educators equate public relations and propaganda. And then wonder why they are not trusted!

"The school district public relations process is a complex, demanding one. It serves in many respects as the conscience of the school district; winning support from internal and external publics alike by seeing that the right thing is done— by demanding the kind of responsible institutional behavior that commands public support.

"Through a planned and systematic two-way process of communication with our internal and external publics, we build morale, goodwill, cooperation and support by letting our constituents and our staff know what our goals are, our achievements and our plans, by getting their reactions, then making adjustments as needed.

"In a nutshell, public relations is a matter of doing the right thing and making sure that people know about it.

"And, public relations is a top-level management responsibility. It deals with the very essence of what our schools are all about and it must receive priority attention."

John H. Wherry
NSPRA Executive Director

Actually, Bernays contends, public relations is the act of "counseling clients on behavior patterns and attitude patterns in order to more effectively meet their goals with the public upon whom they are dependent."

The most important element of good public relations, he says, is the question, "how shall I behave in action and in attitudes to achieve my social objectives?"

School district news releases won't come close to achieving that kind of social responsibility, Bernays continues, but a good, comprehensive public relations program based upon carefully drawn goals and objectives will.

School districts, Bernays says, must "intensify existing favorable attitudes toward education, convert those who are on the fence and negate attitudes that are negative." And it can be done, he says, through "goals, words and actions" embodied in an honest public relations effort.

"Schools don't hesitate to hire accountants or lawyers," Bernays says, "so why shouldn't they hire counsel that understands public relationships—many of which have nothing to do with the teaching process?

"You have to teach the public," he adds, "but you have to deal with the public differently than you do an individual in the classroom."

Begin Today

Thus, the advice of experts in their fields: Don't sit back and wring your hands, bemoaning the fate of education. Get out and argue education's case in your community. Open up two-way communication with your community. Find out your community's aspirations, desires and demands.

Set your goals. Project a "compelling, forward-looking agenda." Accept your social responsibility. Monitor your actions and your behavior. And, defend education as a vital component of American democracy.

Human Relations

One of the old PR maxims goes: "You can't make a silk purse out of a sow's ear."

Obviously, there are some "givens" when you're talking about better public relations. If a school district is mismanaged, and money misspent, and its students poorly educated, all the public relations programs in the world won't do much toward restoring public confidence. If the community is generally ignored except during a financial or other crisis time, the efforts to restore public confidence could require reorganization of the operation of the entire school district.

But, realistically, it is a rare school district that finds itself in such dire circumstances. Most school districts in this country are run by competent, caring professionals: most board of education members either are elected or appointed because they are community members who want to help their schools; and most school districts do have at least a basic community relations programs.

Yet, sometimes we are our own worst enemies.

School boards argue among themselves, and with the community, and many times with the superintendent they hired. Teachers argue with administrators and the school board. Administrators unionize and talk tough and lob verbal hand grenades back at teacher union invectives.

We argue about back-to-basics versus relevant education, about class size and working conditions and fringe benefits, about who is to blame for declining test scores, about accountability and productivity and about vandalism and violence.

We castigate each other over declining enrollments, closing schools, desegregation, politics, bureaucracies, finances, community advisory committees and plenty of other things.

A survey in a large school district once asked all school employees, "If you had a choice, would you have your children attend our schools?" Sixty-one percent said, "No." If that's what employees think of themselves, what does that do to public confidence in their schools?

It's no wonder, then, that education suffers a crisis of public confidence when the public looks at the fishbowl that is eduction today and sees not only rapidly rising taxes but also dissension and disorder among the troops.

The problem here is not mismanagement, but simply human relations. The solution is better interpersonal communication.

Yes, there are bound to be disagreements and a certain amount of internal debate is healthy in any endeavor. But the invective and mistrust that permeates far too much of today's educational establishment is a growing cancer that threatens the very roots of the establishment as it fights to restore the public confidence that once, not too many years ago, was just about unquestioned.

It stands to reason that until education gets its own act together, its job of restoring public confidence is, at best, an uphill struggle.

Perhaps the great Russian writer Fedor Dostoevski summed up the situation when he said:

> "If people around you are spiteful and callous and will not hear you, fall down before them and ask their forgiveness. For, in truth, you have caused them to be as they are."

CHAPTER THREE

Where Do You Stand?

Before we can start building public confidence, before we can improve attitudes, before we can begin making adjustments to make sure our schools are acting in the public interest, we must know where we stand right now.

What is the current level of confidence? What attitudes exist now? How well do our publics feel their interests are being served? Unless we understand where we are starting, we can end up tilting with windmills, chasing shadows, making false assumptions and simply wasting time. On the other hand, once we know where we are strong and where we are weak, we can put our public relations skills to work.

Every community has its own pulse, its own heartbeat, its own likes and dislikes, different feelings and emotions, different causes for agitation and alarm, and different reasons for being satisfied with the status quo. And each community, almost without exception, has some very strong feelings, both pro and con, about its schools.

Critics and Backslappers

School boards and administrators may think they know how their community feels, but rarely do they know. Usually only two small segments of the community take the time to make their thoughts known at the board or administrative level. These are the critics, who waste little time complaining about almost anything, and the backslappers, who smile and praise you and tell you how wonderful everything is.

It is only human nature to dismiss the critics as radicals and to accept the findings of the backslappers. But, in truth, the real pulse of the community usually lies between the stances represented by these two groups.

The secret to building public confidence in education can be stated with disarming simplicity: If we know what the public expects of its schools, and if the public knows that its schools are doing what they expect, public confidence must inevitably follow. Stated another way, we must fulfill public expectations of education if we are to regain public confidence. That is the answer in a nutshell.

The record clearly shows that our schools are doing the best job in our history, or the history of any other country in the world. But somehow the public remains unimpressed, and America's unparalleled social experiment in providing education for everyone is in danger of failing. It is in danger beçause we are losing that which every institution must have in a democratic society—the confidence of the people.

Wherry offers a clear-cut solution to the confidence problem. He believes educators must do four things:

1. Determine what the public now expects of its schools, community by community; determine how public expectations and those of educational leaders differ; and then exercise professional leadership to develop appropriate realistic public expectations.

2. Exercise educational leadership individually and collectively to improve educational performance. Schools earn confidence by their actions, not by their words. We have the best educational system in the world but we know it is still not good enough. We can do better in virtually everything, and we had better be working at that. Hard.

3. Provide the public with adequate information about its schools. That is a basic obligation for every educational institution no matter how large or small. The public will no longer tolerate even a hint that pubic officials are hiding behind one excuse or another (including lack of money) in order to avoid providing them with reasonable information about their schools.

4. Recognize the active role that every school employee—professional or support staff member—plays in providing attitude-forming information to the community and provide training for this staff responsibility.

Summarizing these points another way, we can simply say that our schools must implement total public relations programs. Wherry believes that educators must come to understand that public relations is the practice of social responsibility as Bernays says.

Wherry explains, "As public relations executives, it is our job—we have made a mandate—to become information brokers, to constantly gather facts from surveys and other sources and then aggressively help develop plans to make sure our schools are serving the public interest—that's the heart of public relations—schools.

Different Situations, Different Techniques

One of the best ways to find the pulse of your community is to establish a continuous, 12-month, two-way dialogue with parents, community groups and concerned individuals through a planned program of public relations.

But there is another way for the school district to take its public's pulse—through opinion polls that systematically survey the attitudes of a community toward its schools.

As PR practitioners know, different situations call for different techniques:

☐ We can create attitudes where none exist.

☐ We can intensify existing positive attitudes.

☐ We can convert existing negative attitudes.

☐ We can sometimes negate persistent negative attitudes as well.

But as the growing literature in public relations and social science tells us, the techniques are quite different. They require careful planning and we must know what we are trying to do. We've got to start with a survey. We have to know what the public thinks.

The question we must ask as we consider where to begin the task of building public confidence is, "Do we know where we stand right now in our local communities?

☐ What is the level of confidence?

☐ What attitudes exist now?

☐ How well do our publics feel their interests are being served?

☐ How much do they know?

☐ How much do they want to know?

Wherry says, "I am not advocating school administration by public opinion poll. I am saying that a poll is the place to begin so that we can make effective plans to develop the kinds of attitudes we must have in order for our schools to function effectively."

Basic Questions First

Before your school district takes a survey certain basic questions should be considered. They are:

☐ Will it be a mail-out survey, a carry-home and carry-back survey, a telephone survey, a personal interview or a combination of these?

☐ Is the district asking questions that it can and will respond to with action if necessary? (For example, if parents indicate dissatisfaction with your favorite project, are you willing to change it or dump it? If you aren't, don't ask the question. On the other hand, don't avoid asking questions about issues you know parents are concerned about.)

☐ Do you have an adequate timeline and an adequate budget? Most surveys take about six weeks when done well. Good surveys always cost money, with the price depending upon how the survey is taken.

□ Are you going to surprise the staff, or involve them from the early stages, so they see it as a management tool, not a threat?

□ Who will be responsible for details, and follow-up? If you can afford it, have an outside agency conduct your survey. If not, you can conduct a good survey yourself.

Tips for Conducting a Good Survey

□ The questions should be brief and ask for yes, no, undecided or insufficient information responses. That insufficient information column is extremely helpful. If you are anticipating a finance election, for example, and ask the question, "Do you think your school district spends its money in a reasonable way?" and 40 percent can't answer because they don't have enough information, the work of your election committee is clearly indicated.

□ Keep the total survey short! Perhaps the single biggest mistake of school districts in their surveying is trying to find out how parents feel about everything. Pick out 12 or 15 of the most important issues or concerns and limit yourself to those. Keep the survey to a single page.

□ The first districtwide survey can result in some very disturbing information. An untroubled district may expect that high percentages of parents will support them. Their survey may not reflect that. The general support of parents who respond to community surveys is good, usually above 60 percent, but that is still not as strong as boards and administrators often expect it to be.

Mailed Survey

Once the survey is constructed, you'll have to do advance publicity on the project. A letter should be sent to all those selected to be sampled. This letter will provide background on the survey project and stress its importance. Next, the survey should be mailed with a cover letter. A follow-up postcard reminder should be sent a few days after the survey has been mailed, and then another survey and postcard reminder should be sent to those who have not returned the completed surveys. Despite all this work and cost, it's often difficult to get an adequate response from which you can draw valid conclusions on a mailed survey. You can identify strong trends with some accuracy.

Personal Interview

An alternative technique is the personal interview method of survey research. In this type of survey project, interviewers go to people's homes to ask questions. If you consider this approach, your best bet is to get some help from a consultant or local university. Most school people avoid personal interviewing because the costs are relatively high.

Telephone Survey

A third way to conduct a survey is by telephone. Telephone surveys are relatively inexpensive; have wide geographic reach; and can cover the entire community, missing only those individuals without telephones or with unlisted numbers. Also, call-backs are easy. When someone isn't home, you can place the phone call again. Finally, telephone surveys are fast. If you organize properly, you can complete your survey project in a day or two.

Generally, telephone surveys seem to offer the largest return for school people. About the only practical limitation is the length of the questionnaire—telephone surveys cannot be as long as written surveys or personal interviews.

There are, of course, other considerations in conducting a survey project. For example, the questionnaire must be pretested. This means you should try it out on people just like those who will ultimately be sampled.

Next is the matter of training interviewers or callers. It is important that volunteers have a chance to review and practice the survey.

Even a simple survey will provide you with valuable planning information. When you ask your clients and potential customers what they expect from your program, you're taking the first steps toward successfully marketing what you do.

Once you have the results of your survey, study the percentages carefully. Look for reflected national, statewide and local trends. Some school districts try to tie in their survey questions with the Annual National Gallup Poll on Education. Look for causes of high scores and low ones. Discuss the results with building-level principals, staff and administrators before the results are given to parents, the media and public.

Establish a strategy and a commitment to work on negative areas. Priorities are needed here. Build the strategy into your district's management and accountability plans. On releasing survey results, consider:

☐ A special presentation at an open board meeting, reviewing results and centering around interpretation.

☐ Concurrent with the board release, have news releases ready, covering the same areas. Where results are negative, incorporate the management response. Consider a press briefing. Don't be afraid to

admit that, in some instances, the results are a real concern and
spell out what the district intends to do about them.
□ Have news releases or writing assistance available for building principals who should be encouraged to share the results with their local
community and staff through school-based newsletters, meetings,
etc.

Finally, you should consider polling annually or at least every two years
to see if you have been able to change community opinion through your
efforts following the first survey. You might feel that such a procedure is
expensive, but isn't it better to find out your opinion-changing strategy
isn't working in the first year, than to go on and discover it five years
later?

Marketing Your Schools

A term making the rounds in school PR circles today is that of marketing—the gathering of factual information as to consumer preferences
for goods and services. Marketing, which refers to the process of selling,
can well be applied to the education world much like the business world.
Academic programs, services and facilities that make up the education
students receive are the products of the public schools. The consumers
are the students, parents, taxpayers and business and professional community. School board members, administrators, teachers, other employees and volunteers are the producers.

Bill Banach, administrative assistant for communication services with
the Macomb (Mich.) Intermediate School District, believes it is obvious
that public education must take a new look at the marketplace in which
it does business. "There is a realization in the land that the educational
enterprise must develop new products and services for changing markets,"
he says. While this is hardly news to public relations practitioners it is
still "foreign territory" for too many school administrators and board
members.

Banach says, "Our goal in the Macomb Intermediate School District
is to have schools people want to do business with. Our theme is 'Your
public schools . . . there's no better place to learn.' These words describe
not only what we want the public to think, but what we want the public
schools to be."

Banach believes communication analysis and planning is crucial in the
1980s. "In the past, the focus of educational communication centered on
telling the public what we, as informed professionals, thought they should
know," he explains. The starting point now is to find out more about the
marketplace in which we do business and just what it is our audiences
want and need from their schools. That will be the only way to accom-

modate the new American lifestyle while building a successful understanding and trusting partnership of people.

Banach says the evidence for change is plentiful. For example, the primary market for education has been parents, but only one U.S. adult in three is now a parent. Add to this complications of changing American lifestyles. Today's citizens are increasingly asking, "What's in it for me?" Providing an answer is difficult in most school districts—we don't have products or services enough for parents, and our efforts with adults who don't have children have been minimal.

Banach says there are a number of tools school people can use to work on this job, but the starting point ought to be survey research. This will provide valuable planning information—information that will help assure that the offerings—products and services—are on target.

Do They Know Your Program?

Perhaps the best place to start is by finding out if people know about your program, Banach believes. Then ask them how they found out about what you are offering. These two lines of inquiry will give you a community education "awareness quotient" for your community, and some insights into the channels of communication that are and are not working.

Next, ask people if they have ever participated in a school district program—and if not, why not. Your goal is to find out what's keeping people away. Finally, bounce some new program ideas off people and invite them to offer suggestions. This is called addressing the program to client needs and will assure that your program is in tune with the desires of your constituents.

Of course, you'll also want to add some demographic questions (male/female, length of residence, age of respondent, years of education completed, etc.) to help provide perspective for the answers people give.

Who should be surveyed? The ideal education survey should sample adults in the community who are potential clients of your program. This means finding a list of households from which to draw a sample. (These lists are available from the census program and commercial mailing firms). The key consideration is to make sure that the sample includes all groups who are your school district's potential customers.

A Preschool Marketing Plan
Minnetonka Fights Back

The Minnetonka (Minn.) School District was blanketed with brightly colored flyers appealing to parents to send their children to a private school housed in one of the district's closed elementary buildings.

Newsletters, flyers, invitations, interviews with happily "converted" parents in local newspapers—these were just a few of the aggressive marketing techniques the private schools used to entice Minnetonka area parents.

In the face of this competition, the Minnetonka Public Schools used to just sit back and wring their hands. Public schools didn't "recruit" students according to Judi Mollerus, ASPR, public information coordinator for the school district.

This passive stance might have been tolerable in the original baby boom days, but today there are fewer parents with fewer children. Declining enrollment is causing the layoff of fine teachers. Economies of scale are being lost. Fewer high school courses and alternative programs can be offered because enrollments have dropped below the minimum, according to Mollerus, who wrote about the district's pre-school marketing plan in the July 1985 issue of NSPRA's journal, *Impact.*

In Minnetonka, part of the cause was the declining birth rate, certainly. But there was another critical factor, according to Mollerus. That was the available pool of children. A smaller percentage was coming to the public schools. Private schools took 11 percent of Minnetonka's potential kindergartners in 1978; 17 percent in 1980; and 25 percent in 1983.

And the issue wasn't just one of recruitment. Preschool parents who opted for private schools were negative toward public schools. Half of the private school families in the school district had never enrolled their children in public schools. Although Minnetonka's average basic skills score is in the top 12 percent in the nation and 80 percent of the district graduates go to college, these parents felt negative enough about public schools to decide not even to give them a chance.

"And with our K-12 blinders, we didn't even consider them an audience for communications until they stepped forward at kindergarten registration," Mollerus wrote. "By that time we had lost many of them."

The Minnetonka district decided to fight back with a **marketing approach.** They asked: "What business succeeds if it focuses only on keeping present customers satisfied, without advertising for new ones?"

A survey of area private school parents revealed that they placed a high value on discipline and a warm, caring school environment. The district felt it could make a strong case for public schools on these two points.

An audience analysis was based on information gleaned from two surveys: the annual "first impressions" survey of parents of kindergartners in late September and a telephone survey of private school parents in the spring. The Minnetonka's preschool marketing program was built on these premises:

□ Communicate with preschool parents early and often.

□ Emphasize a caring attitude toward children.

□ Affirm and support parents in their efforts as their children's first "teachers."

□ Encourage an early identification of families with their neighborhood schools.

□ Address kindergarten parents' concerns about transportation and curriculum.

The district used two approaches: direct communications from the school district to preschool parents, plus communications with those judged to be key influences on preschool parents, such as nursery school teachers.

The direct communications with preschool parents included birthday cards for one- and three-year olds, two booklets that tied parent-child activities to the school curriculum and story hours in school libraries for four-year-olds. The district refocused two long-standing events: the health and development screening provided for three-year-olds and the kindergarten registration process.

A new event was added—an orientation and school bus ride for kindergartners and parents in late summer. One principal even issued a polite challenge to parents considering a private kindergarten to visit her school before making a decision.

Communications with the second group, key communicators to preschool parents, were based on establishing ties between nursery school teachers and kindergarten teachers and placing school information in places where preschool parents were likely to see it, such as doctors' waiting rooms.

This intensive marketing campaign began to show results within one year.

□ The first impressions survey yielded many positive comments about the parent-child bus ride, the peppy kindergarten roundup and the new publications.

□ Minnetonka's kindergarten enrollment increased at the same time the number of students in private kindergartens in the area declined. The percentage of kindergarten students in private schools dropped from 25 to 19 percent after one year of the marketing effort.

Mollerus said that the preschool marketing program was by far the most ambitious, comprehensive public relations effort the Minnetonka Schools had ever undertaken. As they examined the reasons for its success, they identified four factors to duplicate in future programs.

1. The Preschool Marketing Program communicates that the district staff has confidence in themselves. They believe that their schools are worth "selling."

2. Communications should be frequent, sustained and based on both the written word and personal contacts.

3. Current parents, our "satisfied customers," should be actively involved.

4. Principals, teachers and administrators have adopted a "**marketing mindset.**" They evaluate every idea for preschool outreach on the basis of how the parents of small children will perceive the message and react to it.

(For additional information contact the Minnetonka Public Schools, 261 School Avenue, Excelsior, MN 55331).

CHAPTER FOUR

Where Do You Start?

School systems have public relations, good or bad . . . for better or for worse, whether they like it or not. Too many school districts looking to develop a public relations program fail to realize that they already have one, and it may be a disaster.

In fact, a school system is a communications system, made up of staff members and students who day in and day out are sending messages (often unknowingly) to a wide variety of publics.

Each day, your district interacts with its local community. Secretaries greet visitors to your buildings. Bus drivers meet parents and students at dawn, and share local roadways throughout the day. Teachers deal directly with "clients" of the district—students—and their parents. The switchboard operator may speak with as many community members as all other staff combined.

PR and the Management Team

Wise school administrators know that they've got to manage their communications before their communications manage them. That's what school public relations is all about. Like it or not, these daily events can do as much (or as little) for your district as 10 full-page photo spreads in the daily newspaper.

The problem, then, is not really starting a public relations program. It's doing a better job with the one you have. And that takes one major ingredient: commitment. For years, school administrators have said that public relations is important. Unfortunately, many didn't do much more than say it.

It takes active commitment—not just passive acceptance—from the board of education, the superintendent, from the other top administrators and from the principals and teachers in each school building.

School public relations is defined by the National School Public Relations Association as a planned and systematic two-way process

**of communications between an educational organization and its
internal and external publics designed to build morale, goodwill,
understanding and support for that organization.**

Larry Ascough, director of public relations for the Dallas (Texas)
Schools, believes that school public relations is a key part of the management process. "If you're going to achieve the district's goals, you've got
to see that citizens and employees are informed and involved," Ascough
says.

> "If you want to keep your district's programs on track and be responsive to
> public needs and concerns . . . if you want to keep a finger on the pulse of
> the community and the school system and improve your decision-making
> . . . you've got to have a two-way communications system. In short, you
> can't manage effectively—at least, not for very long—without good school
> public relations."

And, after commitment comes analysis. What does your community
really think of you? What do they want from you? Do you have a board
policy on communication and public relations? Do you have in-service
courses to help your staff deal more effectively with their many publics?

Since every school system, and the schools and communities within
them, is different, public relations programs have to be individualized to
meet local needs. Planning and maintaining a program is the responsibility of management at all levels.

These are the kinds of questions that must be asked. As discussed in
the previous chapter, you need a clear picture produced by public opinion
analysis. You must know what your community expects of education,
what your community's knowledge or ignorance is of education, and what
your community's hopes, aspirations and desires are as to the education
program for their students.

Getting Organized To Begin

Then, armed with this knowledge, Bernays says, "You must define
your goals in as simple terms as the Ten Commandments or the Four
Freedoms or the 14 Points." Also, he says, "you have to define them on
the basis of the three time elements that go into goals: short-term, intermediate and long-term.

Of primary importance, he continues, is the need to "get away from
hunch, to use sound procedures based on fact-finding and socially sound
goals."

The school public relations planning process, Bernays says, should
involve the following:

1. A statement of goals,
2. A statement of research pertaining to the goals,

3. A statement of school district reorientation that must be accomplished in light of the research and new goals,
4. A definition of the strategy you are going to use in accomplishing your goals and
5. The timing of your tactics to accomplish your goals.

You must have a systems outline, he says, in which "you write a drama that hasn't happened yet, in which every step of the drama, every appearance of every actor, every scene is outlined . . . yet, all are subject to change."

Some Whys and Wherefores

NSPRA recommends that the following five key points be considered by each school board as it develops its own communications policy statement.

1. The educational organization should commit to writing a clear and concise policy statement with respect to its public information program.
2. The policy statement should be approved through formal action by the governing board of the organization, should be published in its policy manual and should be reviewed by the governing board annually.
3. The policy statement should express the purposes of the organization's public information program and provide the delegation of such authority to the executives of the organization as necessary to achieve the objectives.
4. The provisions of the policy statement should be made known to the entire staff or membership of the organization through all appropriate means.
5. Commitment to the achievement of the purposes of the organization's public information policy should be demonstrated through the allocation of adequate human and financial resources to the public information program.

School systems should draft policies that will support:
□ Establishment of a communication and community relations program for the district,
□ A news policy based upon honesty, openness and fairness,
□ Recognition of the schools as an integral part of the community,
□ The concept that institutions, including schools, are built and improved through shared ideas, not only within the system,
□ The formation of advisory groups,
□ The participation of parents and other community resources in school programs,

☐ A rational plan and procedures for community use of school facilities and grounds,

☐ Guidelines for distribution of materials, the conduct of promotions and contests and soliciting of funds from school personnel or students,

☐ Communication between and among governmental agencies, and

☐ A plan for communication in the event of a disaster.

Guidelines for a Board Policy

Pauline Radebaugh, member of the Columbus (Ohio) Board of Education, believes school trustees have two main responsibilities in the area of school public relations:

☐ To build a strong public relations department in your school district.

☐ To use that public relations department effectively as you carry out your board duties. Radebaugh offers these tips for building a strong public relations department:

☐ Recognize the value a strong, effective PR department holds for your school system.

☐ Remember that part-time employees can deliver only part-time PR.

☐ Fill your PR positions with individuals who have training or experience working as public relations professionals, not as English teachers or librarians.

☐ Respect the professionalism and acknowledge the expertise of PR people as you do other members of your district's staff.

☐ Support the involvement of your PR staff in professional development opportunities.

☐ Make sure that your district's organization chart allows for your PR department to have a direct link to the superintendent.

☐ Recognize the valuable role the head of your PR department can play in overall school operations and districtwide decisions by requesting that he or she be a member of your superintendent's cabinet.

☐ Support the operational needs of your PR department by requesting that all department and major project budgets include a separate line item covering work required from the PR department.

Getting a Formal Program Underway

Check your state laws. Many legislatures have done some of the preliminary legwork for you. Sunshine laws and open public meeting acts may have mandated some of the kinds of communication that public bodies in your state must prepare.

Prepare a formal district policy for your board of education to approve. It should include:

☐ Reasons for adopting the policy;

☐ What the policy is designed to do;

☐ General means of implementation;

☐ Delegation of the responsibility for the program from the board to the chief administrator or designate and

☐ Provisions for periodic evaluation.

The policy, once passed, should be duplicated and distributed throughout the school or district and its community.

Balance These Four

A good school-community relations program balances four characteristics:

1. **Two-way communication.** A good PR program includes listening as much as talking. Column inches of newspaper space and minutes of radio or television time are important, but public relations based on what's happening is more important.

2. **For all people.** Employees, students, and teachers—the internal publics—are as important as editors, legislators and Rotarians. In fact, a well-informed internal public can serve as several thousand extra eyes, ears and mouthpieces in the community.

3. **Systematic.** Use of the newspaper to the exclusion of all other media won't get the message across. Community newsletters alone won't work, either. The communication specialist must systematically identify each segment of the public and decide upon the best medium to use to communicate with each—print, radio/TV, group meetings, etc.

4. **Continuous.** School PR is a year-round operation. How strange it is that the same school that's been sunshine and roses for three years and nine months could spontaneously and coincidentally crumble into its foundation for the three months around bond issue approval time. A good communications program says "good" when there's good and "problem" when there are problems.

Allocate the Necessary Resources

The most creative, innovative and wide-reaching board policy will be useless without proper support to carry it out. Too often, public relations becomes responsibility #41 added to the job description of an already-

Guidelines for Setting Up a School District Public Relations Program

1. Board members should recognize that citizens have a right to know what is happening in their school system; that board members and central office staff have an obligation to see that all publics are kept systematically and adequately informed and that the school system will benefit from seeing that citizens get all information, good and bad, directly from the system itself.

2. A committee should be appointed by the board that includes board members, staff members and community experts in the field of communication. The group should be large enough to brainstorm all ideas, but not so large as to be hampered by the number of members.

3. This committee must develop a proposed policy statement for the school board which will commit the system to development of a program for open com-

munications with its various publics. The statement should be broad enough to serve as the goals of the public relations program for the system.

4. Once the policy statement has been adopted and publicized, the committee should develop guidelines for work which will include what their final report to the board will cover, and a timeline for activities.

5. A person with strong, professional communication skills should be placed in charge of the main research and development procedures as directed by the committee.

6. The committee should secure workable background information on what is being done in the area of school public relations around the country, and then make an assessment of what is being done in their own system. This analysis should include an evalua-

overworked administrator. Consequently, the PR assignment gets a when-I-get-around-to-it priority.

Best, of course, is the employment of a full-time educational communication specialist. NSPRA maintains a personnel clearinghouse for such PR professionals.

tion of all communication presently being used.

7. Using the policy statement adopted by the board, the committee should develop goals for open communication between the school system and its internal and external publics. These goal statements will form the basis of the public relations program and will be used in the selection of the activities to be initiated the first year.

8. An initial list of many different techniques for communicating with both the internal and external publics of the school system should be developed to insure a systematic way of meeting the systemwide goals. These publics will include obvious ones such as the parents, taxpayers, community business leaders, ministers, non-parents and teachers, as well as other important ones such as secretaries, bus drivers, lunchroom workers, custo-dians and maintenance workers.

9. The committee's report to the board should contain the proposed goal's statements of the public relations program and the activities which will help meet those goals. It should be organized in such a way that there is little doubt how communication can be initiated. Provisions must be made for both an adequate staff and adequate funding to insure the success of the program. Accountability procedures should be included so that the results of the program can be carefully analyzed.

10. The basic staff should include an efficient, reliable secretary and a professional communication specialist. (Larger systems will require expanded staffs with specific skills in different areas—writing, graphics, in-service training, media relations, etc.)

NSPRA also conducts an annual seminar to train and to update the skills of district communication specialists and school principals, administrators, board members and superintendents. In addition, the association also conducts staff development workshops to improve the communication skills of administrators, principals, teachers, board of eduction members, parents and support staff members, for local districts or regional groups.

If a full-time PR specialist seems out of the question to start, consider part-time help. Often, a graduate student in educational PR or in journalism can arrange for an internship at your school. Perhaps a local reporter or a retired person could help. Or a journalism or English teacher could be given a reduced teaching load to take on added PR responsibilities.

Clerical help is required, too. It's "pennywise but pound foolish" to pay a specialist to perform routine duplicating, collating and envelope-stuffing. Work-study students or a business/typing class might help. New technology is cutting time and money in many ways. Electronic word processing equipment is discussed in a future chapter.

PR Programs Are Not Frills

As early as the late 1970s the Pennsylvania School Boards Assn. (PSBA) issued a special report which said "PR Programs Are Not Frills." The work of a 32-member commission, sponsored by PSBA to develop recommendations for "strengthening the working relationships of school boards and superintendents" and composed of school board members, district superintendents, and intermediate unit administrators from across the state, included the following statement:

Communications

The commission believes that an elected school board, and the administrators hired to carry out public policy, have a mandate to communicate to all citizens.

The commission believes that planned, organized and effective communications are essential if the school's employees are to perform their assigned tasks as effectively and efficiently as possible. Effective school management and communication responsibilities cannot be separated. The commission asserts that improved understanding between school officials and the community-at-large hinges directly on the working relationship between the board and the superintendents. The relationship of the local school board to government and its place in the governmental structure are important considerations in school board operations. An understanding of this relationship contributes to more effective leadership and communication by the local board.

Governing boards of school districts are generally one of the largest (if not the largest) employers in local communities. The news media cannot satisfy the total communication needs that such an employer requires to ensure that the district operates efficiently and effectively on a day-to-day basis. The commission supports the position, therefore, that planned communication programs (requiring some public expenditures) which can be supported, evaluated and measured, provide a long-term benefit for students. Such programs are not frills. The commission feels that honest, straightforward, two-way communication programs between local school officials and their constituents are absolutely necessary in retaining public confidence and support for public schools.

The commission, therefore, recommends that:

□ Boards should have an approved and responsible communications policy which is shared with, and understood by, the school-community.

□ School districts should prepare a board-superintendent brochure and other handouts for public board meetings which include, for example, legal requirements of the board and the superintendent's office, meeting dates and times, and how the public may address the board.

□ Boards and superintendents should develop a staff newsletter which goes to all employees in order that the staff has an opportunity to better understand board-superintendent business and operations.

□ School boards should establish guidelines and responsibility for communication with the news media on a regular and on-going basis.

□ Boards should establish communication systems that will provide responsive feedback between the board and its various publics.

□ School boards should provide an annual report to the community explaining the school district's programs, services and its progress.

What About the Cost?

Wherry points out, "The argument sometimes offered that a school district just can't afford a public relations program falls apart pretty quickly when you consider how much staff time is already being spent on public relations activities."

According to a study conducted in New Jersey, an average of 37 percent of the superintendent's time was spent in communication or public relations-related activities, Wherry says. "You also need to consider that at least the same percentage of time is spent on PR by school principals, and that teachers spend at least 10 percent of their time on PR by even the narrowest definition of the term. School secretaries, including telephone time and other communication activities, are spending 60 percent of their time on public relations by conservative estimates, and other support staff members, including custodians, food service employees, bus drivers and maintenance personnel, also spend a surprising amount of time communicating with each other, students, parents and the general public as well."

"The fact is," Wherry explains, "if we would compute the percentage of each employee's time spent in public relations and multiply that by their annual salary, we would find that we are already spending a great deal on public relations. The question really is, are we getting our money's worth? A coordinated school district public relations program can make the money we are already spending on PR much more effective."

A Climate of Commitment

A deep, obvious commitment to PR on the part of the chief school administrator is essential. "An administrator" asking for input and assistance from the faculty and staff is one thing. But "the administrator" emphasizing the importance of PR can motivate even the most reluctant employee. "Tokenism" is quickly identified and programs without this commitment are in trouble from the start. The superintendent and school board set the tone for the entire school system.

The communication specialist must be included as a key member of the administrative cabinet, reporting directly to the chief school administrator. Many decisions made by district administrators have direct communication ramifications. Budget and bond campaigns, test score results, textbook censorship, busing plans—all are topics with important communication angles. Proper preparation of the community by the communication specialist could help prevent embarrassing headlines later and reduce the feeling within the community that the school is "putting something over on them."

Also, the communication specialist will maintain close contact with representatives of the local news media. Reporters frequently need to contact the chief school administrator on an urgent or fast-breaking story. In such cases, the communication specialist needs direct access to the superintendent for fast, accurate responses to meet media deadlines. If reporters can't get the facts quickly from school officials, they'll get them from somewhere else—possibly incorrectly.

Know the Media and Community

The public relations specialist should know the media representatives. Buy and read all the local newspapers. Listen to all the radio and television stations. One at a time, visit individual editors and station managers to find out how the schools can help them. You'll find this approach is a lot more successful than asking how they can help you. The communication specialist should give media representatives his or her home telephone number in case they need a school spokesperson after hours. Unfortunately, all news doesn't break between 8:30 a.m. and 4:30 p.m. five days a week, and it's far better to give accurate facts at midnight than waken to blazing headline mistakes in the morning.

Meet the community. Take a look at your community in general. Get a copy of the most recent census taken in the area. See if a demographic study has ever been done. Look in the files to see what communication tools have been tried in the past, and which were successful.

Identify and analyze the power base—both formal and informal. Does the PTA president hold the power, or does the woman who sits in the back of the room really make all the decisions? The difference could be important.

Cultivate the most influential community members into a group of "Key Communicators." Collect the names of people who are active, respected and listened-to in your community. Seek out their input on various school policies. Show them that the school is interested in hearing from the community. Produce a steady flow of school district information—brochures, newsletters, bulletins—for them. You'll get accurate input from the community and you'll win new "friends" for the schools.

Then, when a crisis occurs, you've got a core of respected community leaders who can help get information out to the public quickly and accurately.

CHAPTER FIVE

Working with Parents and Students

Too often, the parent is taken for granted, the parent-teacher conference is a pro forma exercise, parents' night accomplishes little, and parents go away mad.

In its report, the National Commission on Excellence in Education emphasized the role of parents in the reform of the education system when it said:

"Your vigilance and your refusal to be satisfied with less than the best are the imperative first steps. But your right to a proper education for your children carries a double responsibility. You must be a living example of what you expect your children to honor and to emulate and you bear a responsibility to participate actively in your child's education."

Undoubtedly, the answer to many of the problems facing the schools is parent involvement. Rapidly, it is becoming almost axiomatic that wherever you find a really successful educational program—regardless of the standards used in the evaluation—you will also find a strong, expanding program of parent involvement.

Unfortunately, for many parents, life today has become increasingly complicated as they try to juggle the demands of a job and the drive for personal fullfillment with the responsibilities of child rearing. This "balancing act" is necessary because more mothers today hold jobs outside the home. About 56 percent of women with children between the ages of three and six are now working.

Wayne Holder, director of child protection for the American Humane Assn., was quoted in a national magazine interview, "Families have become a group of individuals who each get on their own track at 7:30 in the morning and get off of it at night. Children don't receive enough adult interaction. The face-to-face discussion of feelings, values and philosophy of life between parents and children is missing completely."

Single Parents

In some schools, as many as 90 percent of the children are from single-parent families. In others, the statistics may be lower, but according to U.S. Bureau of the Census figures, nearly one-fifth of the nation's children will live part of their school-age life with a single parent. Principals and teachers need to work together to build recognition of this into all school activities.

The stereotype of the single parent is powerful. It's usually a mother, working at a full-time job while trying to keep the home together, leaving her little time to help the children with their schoolwork. Some teachers accept the stereotype, but others know better, and they actively involve single parents in their children's learning at home.

In fact, the amount and quality of single-parent help is comparable to that of two-parent homes, according to the Center for Social Organization of Schools at The Johns Hopkins University. Its research shows that those teachers who foster the single parent stereotype are those who do not actively seek any parental involvement at all. "When we look at teachers who actually attempt to involve parents," said research scientist Joyce Epstein, "we find that they get as much help from single parents as from two-parent families."

In a study involving 82 teachers and 1,269 parents in 11 school districts in Maryland, Epstein found that single parents spent more minutes helping their children at home than did two-parent families, while the latter spent more time helping at the school.

Children Without Supervision

Even more worrisome for parents is the fact that millions of children are left on their own after school. The Children's Defense Fund, a Washington group, says that about 5.2 million children 13 and under whose parents are employed full time are without supervision for significant parts of the day. Such youngsters are likely to get into trouble.

Children are suffering in other ways, too. While instances of parental abuse of youngsters are still the exception, experts point to a disturbing epidemic of cases involving brutal beatings or sexual attacks.

Stories of sexual abuse of children have suddenly become commonplace and have given educators perhaps their most delicate challenge. What is the role of the school in alerting children to the hazards? How can the school teach the children to avoid potentially dangerous situations—without frightening them to the point where they shun normal contacts?

Tips for Working With Single Parents

□ Hold a staff in-service training session on working with single parents. Many staff members are themselves single parents, and can share some of their concerns and problems. Awareness needs to be built first, then a discussion of ways to alleviate problems.

□ Establish single-parent groups so that they can discuss concerns. Remember to schedule these sessions at various times so that both working parents and those staying at home can participate. It is best to consider different times of the day. Provide baby-sitting services for parents who need this help.

□ Remind parent groups that prizes are not given for children who bring both parents to a meeting.

□ Be extremely sensitive to teachers and administrators who might use the term "broken home," "fractured family" and "diminished family" to produce a stereotyped attitude about the special children involved.

□ Schedule parent meetings, parent-teacher conferences, and other possible activities in the morning before parents need to be on the job, or in the evening, after work, or on the weekend. This is important for single parents and for two-career parents. Many parents want to volunteer and share in the school activities, but their work schedule doesn't enable them to attend activities during certain hours. Don't penalize the mother who is simply not available from 8 a.m. to 4 p.m. as "unwilling to help." Plan for ways that mother/father can contribute later.

□ Develop special programs for latchkey children. Arrange to have the school open early and close late. Seek volunteers from the community and parents. Latchkey programs providing extended day care for children are increasing. Financial support can come from local business, churches, chambers of commerce, etc.

□ Provide space on school forms for names and addresses of both parents, and for names of blended family members if the parents re-marry. Provide duplicate sets of school materials if requested.

Child Abuse Prevention

A theater group in British Columbia came up with one answer at the request of a parent group and it is spreading across Canada. "Feeling Yes, Feeling No" is the name of a child abuse prevention program developed by the Green Thumb Theatre in Vancouver, which has also been shown to more than 8,000 children in 46 schools in Manitoba by the Actors' Showcase. Reportedly, the program successfully walks the fine line between instruction and sensation and has been received enthusiastically by parents and children alike.

The program uses a combination of dramatic sketches and discussion to teach children how to identify YES and NO feelings, how to recognize and avoid dangerous situations, and how to talk to adults about unpleasant things that happen to them. The program does not teach sexuality or solicit disclosures from children. To keep each session on the track parent and staff workshops are given before the children see the program.

The scripts for grades 1-3 and grades 4-6 are identical in content and structure except that the setting for one is a candy store, which becomes a movie theater for the older group. YES feelings are identified as those that come from touches that make one feel good, while NO feelings are "touches you want to stop, that make you feel angry, confused or frightened."

The script is carefully structured with progressive building blocks of information. The children learn: "If you feel NO, say no. If you are left with a NO feeling, tell an adult you trust. Sometimes you have to say NO even though it's hard. Keep telling adults until someone listens and helps you."

The last point is particularly important, says Donna McLennan, program coordinator. "It isn't uncommon for a sexually abused child to tell up to nine adults before he or she is finally believed." Many districts are purchasing or producing special parent booklets providing suggested ways parents can discuss child abuse with their children and steps to take to protect themselves

More widespread than outright abuse is the psychological trauma for many youngsters in families affected by divorce, separation and out-of-wedlock births. By the time they become adults, close to half of today's youngsters are expected to have spent part of their childhood with just one parent.

Latch-key Programs Help

Communities are today coming up with a variety of ways to provide extra support for latch-key children (those coming and going from empty homes) and their parents.

The National School Public Relations Assn. has published a booklet called *It's 3 O'Clock . . . And Time to Help Children on Their Own.* It's designed to be sent home to parents to help them and their children "plan wisely so the time at home alone will be spent safely and usefully." One of its many valuable recommendations is to post conspicuously the "Rules of the House," covering such items as these:

"Rules of Our House"

□ Go straight home without delay. Don't delay or go to anybody else's house unless you get permission before leaving school. Don't speak with strangers on the way home or go to someone else's house.

□ Always keep the door locked when you are in the house.

□ Always answer the telephone and respond to somebody at the door—without unlocking it. Keep all conversations very brief.

□ Don't allow anybody in the door unless you have permission beforehand for that person to be inside.

□ Never tell anybody at the door or on the phone that you're home alone. Say your parents are busy and that you'll take a message for them to call back. Then hang up or leave the door immediately.

□ If you have friends at home when adults are away (this needs to be discussed and agreed upon), let them know they must agree to "house rules." Never allow them to do things in your home that you are forbidden to do, no matter what they say their parents allow.

□ If you come home and a door is open or a window is broken, or anything else makes you think that somebody might be there, do not go inside. Go to a neighbor's house and call Mom or Dad or the police. Be sure to give your address completely and clearly.

The Ardsley Union Free School District in Westchester County, N.Y., leased unused classroom space to a non-profit child care center, thus easing the district's declining enrollment problem and providing a community service as well. Some districts, such as Galloway, N.J., have taken on the service themselves. Galloway initiated a program at two elementary schools last September, providing snacks, homework supervision, puppet shows, games and counseling for a cost to parents that averages $1.60 an hour.

In some areas where after-school programs aren't available, phone lines are being used with success. "Phone-Friend" was initiated in 1982 by Pennsylvania State U. in two small area communities. Prevention-oriented, it has since spread to about 10 sites in the nation, said Louise Guerney, associate professor of human development and training director for the service. The line serves as a "friend" children can turn to and a way to create community awareness of children's needs, she said.

What started out as a program to teach students at one South Carolina elementary school how to take care of themselves in emergency situations turned into a curriculum now in use by schools in 35 states and several foreign countries.

"Housewise-Streetwise," developed by teachers, principals, parents and child advocates in Greenville County, is a six-day program to teach 7-9-year-olds "survival" skills such as what to do if someone touches them, how to make emergency calls, whom to go to for help and how to avoid dangerous situations, said Jayne Crisp, director of the county Victim Witness Assistance Programs.

Joint Custody and Schools

With the growing trend of marital separation and divorce, there is a need for parents to care for children in alternative ways. One of these ways is "joint custody."

Joint custody is a method of defining responsibilities for the children of a marriage where separation has occurred. The parents work out a contract, independently or with a lawyer, which more or less spells out parenting responsibilities.

The areas which are dealt with include financial responsibilities, allotment of time and place, general obligations around school activities, health issues, and child-care responsibilities. In theory these should be shared equally. That seems to be an ideal which is difficult to achieve, but is an improvement over the responsibilities of one-parent custody.

How will all of this affect the classroom teacher? This can be determined by the effect it has on children. No child remains unaffected by a change in family structure no matter what that is. In most cases, children seem to weather the problems of separation and divorce. Joint custody is a creative way to help this happen. What can teachers do to help support these children?

When a child isn't prepared for school, a firm but sensitive approach from the teacher helps. If this becomes a chronic problem, parents need to know. Teachers should feel free to communicate with either parent. It is the responsibility of the parents to amiably reach some kind of solution.

Another help is for teachers to take time to really listen to the concerns of the child. Teachers can represent a caring adult in the middle of an otherwise difficult situation. This is an extra step to go, but can pay dividends in the child's academic achievement.

But teachers need help in handling such cases and more and more school districts are developing special in-service programs to build teaching skills to handle this new family structure.

Factors for Successful Parent Involvement

An analysis of effective parent participation programs in six counties of New Jersey identified *five common factors* that seem to accompany success. They were outlined in the February 1982 issue of *Interact*, published by the New Jersey State Department of Education.

1. Climate. A warm, caring atmosphere seemed to pervade those programs that worked. The methods varied, but the impact was the same: the school was saying, "Welcome! We're glad you're here. This is done by making sure that the staff (including the receptionist and other office workers) who meet parents give them the VIP treatment instead of seeing them as intruders.
2. Relevance. Programs were based on what parents cared about, which involved surveys to learn their interests: whether they only wanted to talk with other parents, participate as volunteers or take workshops to improve relations with their children and help them with their school work.
3. Convenience. Successful programs make it easier for parents to participate by dealing with the factors that keep them home. This could mean car pools, buses or vans for those who have no transportation, providing child care or special activities for the children the parents must bring.
4. Publicity. Let people know what you have planned. Attractive flyers and posters all over town can boost upcoming events. The most effective are personal invitations via the telephone.
5. Commitment. A successful parent-involvement program is time-consuming. It demands time and commitment on the part of the principal and his total staff. Considering the payoff in parent and community support, the issue is "Can schools afford NOT to provide successful parent programs?"

The Parent-Teacher Conference

A good way to improve parent-school relationships is with the parent-teacher conference. Successful parent-teacher conferences require considerable planning for teachers and parents if both are to provide input and both are to take away some new information about a particular child. When that happens, the best communication can take place—two people face to face, each speaking and listening to the other, each asking questions. For many parents, this is their only contact with the school.

Some school systems hold a mini-workshop for their staff where veteran teachers hold role-playing conferences and discuss how to react to particular situations. If you ask for volunteers, you are more likely to get those who are comfortable with conferences. The others, as well as new teachers, can observe and then react.

Tips for Parent/Teacher Conference

☐ Begin on a positive note and listen closely and sympathetically. You'll learn things that will help you deal with each child.

☐ Get away from your desk and sit at a small conference table or student desk so there isn't a barrier between you and the parent.

☐ Be prepared—gather records such as grade sheets, papers and other examples of student work, test results or even notes passed.

☐ Jot down the main points you want to get across to parents, translating "pedagese" into simple language. Try to be specific.

☐ Focus on solutions which you and the parent arrive at jointly. Concentrate on one or two areas rather than sending parents away with a bushel of questions.

If parent-teacher conferences are to be well attended, they should be held at times when parents can come to school without too much inconvenience. Because more and more children come from families with working parents, schools are rapidly changing the hours they set aside for conferences. Many now schedule time before school (or the parent's job) starts and in the evening and on Saturdays. Some districts supply a substitute for the teacher who has a heavy schedule of conferences outside "normal" working hours. And, the new scheduling techniques have resulted in an increased number of fathers attending the meetings.

Some school districts have gone even a step further by seeking volunteers to serve as adult advocates to check on the progress of students whose parents are unable—or unwilling—to come to school and offer encouragement to their child.

Helping the Parent Communicate

A wise school district also helps parents prepare for the parent-teacher conference, too, for an unprepared parent can make the conference almost as unproductive as can an uninformed teacher.

Through newsletters, PTA meetings, features in local newspapers and even TV and radio programs, some school districts emphasize this point, and help parents prepare for a truly productive parent-teacher meeting.

Toward the end of the conference parents should review with the teacher some of the action points discussed that might help the child do better. This might include such things as possible remedial work, improved study habits, revised goals, more understanding, outside reading, more credit being given for strengths, etc.

Tip for Parents and Child After the Conference

☐ Discuss the conference with your child. First, point out strengths. Then talk about the areas that need improvement.

☐ Start immediately on any action you have decided to take. Did the teacher recommend books for you or your child to read? Is there a better arrangement for studying at home? Is outside help needed in a special area? Begin at once to follow through with the plan you and the teacher decided upon.

☐ Feel free to call the school if you wish to check on your child's progress or if you think another conference is needed. Teachers generally value such interest on the part of parents.

☐ Make certain your child understands that you and the teacher are working together; that you and the teacher are in partnership, with the sole aim of helping him/her get the best education possible.

How Did We Do?

Finally, all parent-teacher conferences should be evaluated. One Pennsylvania school system gives parents leaving a conference a three-part questionnaire, asking: "Did the conference accomplish what you had hoped it would? What was the most effective part of the conference? What would you like to see done differently the next time to improve the conference?"

Using such evaluations techniques, parent-teacher conferences can be constantly restructured to meet the concerns of parents.

Making Parents Partners

Another "better way" of parent involvement is the Parent Partnership Program which the Philadelphia Public Schools established several years ago. The program was aimed at achieving greater parental participation in the education of their children. It included six components:

1. **Parent Workshops**—Monthly meetings are held throughout the school system which are designed to assist parents to become more

effective in the total education of their children (especially pre-school children) by helping to acquire an understanding of the various aspects of child development and to help parents recognize, make and use learning materials in the home.

2. **Books for Tots**—This component provides parents of every pre-school child in the city with books and other printed materials to foster the development of reading and reading-related skills in the home and to introduce young children to age-appropriate reading materials.

3. **Student Tutor Corps**—Older children provide tutorial help in the development and strengthening of basic skills of young children. Tutoring sessions occur throughout the city in private certified day care homes.

4. **Radio-TV Programs**—Programs are presented on public and commercial stations as well as closed-circuit in the schools. The presentations are designed to provide examples of educational/instructional activities that parents may participate in with their children while at home.

5. **Special Education Center**—The Center houses instructional materials and information geared for parents of children eligible for school district special education programs. Trained personnel at the Center assist parents in the development of materials and activities for use with handicapped children at home as well as provide immediate counseling services for parents. Periodic workshops in each district offer opportunities to "tailor" information, materials, and counseling services to the specific needs of parents of handicapped children.

6. **Public Awareness**—A coordinated program to inform parents of school-age children and the community at large about the variety of Parent Partnership Program activities through print and broadcast media, and respond to individual inquiries about the program by providing printed information and sample materials tailored to specific personal requests.

Each component of the Parent Partnership Program was developed and operated at no additional cost to the school district. Many school district staff members contributed their time and effort to the Parent Partnership Program as a demonstration of their commitment to working with parents for the benefit of children.

Schools Are Students

Schools are students. The story of schools is the story of students and their accomplishments. Unfortunately, the minority of students get the majority of school publicity—publicity which creates a negative public attitude toward students and schools. Our job, as school communicators and administrators, is to turn this attitude around. Our best allies are the majority of students.

Since the *At Risk* report, school districts across the country have been bringing student achievements to the community's attention in positive ways, including the following:

☐ **An Excellence Fair.** Five small Denver suburban school districts and teacher associations in Adams County, Colo., have successfully involved community leaders and senior citizens in an educational excellence fair, held in a shopping mall large enough to showcase the districts. As a major promotional activity for the Fair, an essay contest was conducted for students in grades 3-8. Prizes of $50 savings bonds and reference books were awarded to the winners in each district during the Fair.

☐ **Pride Week Campaign.** In the face of the challenges and stresses confronting schools today, the community and staff members sometimes lose sight of how good their schools really are. The Roseville (Minn.) Area Schools, District 623, decided to celebrate their successes by proclaiming "Proud to be in 623" week. The purpose of the celebration was to improve staff morale, to promote a feeling of pride among staff, students and community members for the high quality schools in District 623, and to honor 25-year employees. Activities included outdoor signs and shopping center marquees carrying the message, "Proud to be in 623—we're proud of our schools," special programs and open houses, extensive radio and television news coverage and a staff social.

☐ **Texas Academic Decathlon.** A "tournament of minds" placing scholarship on a par with muscle, the Texas Academic Decathlon brings students from all over the state together to compete in a contest of academic strength.

According to E.A. Sigler of the Highland Park (Texas) public schools, the purposes of the Academic Decathlon are to encourage students to develop a greater respect for knowledge; to promote wholesome interschool competition in academic areas of study and interest; to stimulate intellectual growth and achievement and to encourage public interest and awareness of outstanding programs in the schools.

Training in PR

The Forest Hills school system in Cincinnati, Ohio, sponsors a Student News Network that allows students to gain writing experience through a news gathering and reporting network. Students selected to participate in the program are given assignments to cover specific events. Their articles are then edited by an adult, and submitted to the two local newspapers for publication. Students are paid minimum wage for the time spent at the event and in writing the first draft of the news release.

A similar program has operated in the Randolph (Mass.) public schools, where students are trained in several public relations and communications capacities and actively take part in the school system's public relations program as they learn. Training is provided in:

☐ Radio and television broadcasting; writing scripts for spot announcements; conducting interviews; arranging for guests to be interviewed,

☐ Writing news releases for local papers,

☐ Arranging for special projects to be displayed in: supermarkets, banks, stores, and libraries, and

☐ Working on promotional campaigns; community service organizations such as Heart Fund; organizing and interesting citizens in school-related programs, and creating original bumper stickers for projects.

Student Advisory Council: An Important Link

One of the Lincoln (Neb.) schools' most important communications links to the community in the past has been a student advisory council.

Here's how it works:

The superintendent's student advisory council consists of representatives from each of the district's four high schools and an alternative school. Each school sends two members of its student council (frequently the president), the editor of the student newspaper and a fourth member at large. Student councils are free to select the at-large member and are encouraged to select a student who is not already in a leadership role or one who is representing the noninvolved or antischool members of the student body. The alternative school students simply elect a representative since they are a small school and have neither a student council nor a student newspaper.

The council meets every other week, usually in the evening. Occasionally, there is a breakfast meeting and usually in the early fall and again in the late spring, the council is entertained at the superintendent's home.

The council operates with a minimum of procedural regulations. The director of student activities, a central office staff member, acts as executive secretary, keeping minutes, sending out agendas, etc. The superintendent chairs the meetings, which take the form of informal discussions of reports brought to the council. When votes are required, each school is allowed one vote.

The agenda includes items that students have listed as their concerns, reports from the superintendent with requests for advice or opinions, and opportunity for students to exchange reports on activities at their building. Although the council is not a working committee in the sense that it conducts programs of its own, it provides leadership for such projects as interschool visitations, registering student voters and improvement of interschool sportsmanship.

Children With Problems

But all students are not involved in school activities. Many are on the very brink of dropping out of school. They reflect a host of problems which have never before confronted teachers and school administrators. Handling these problems has required school leaders to develop a number of special programs targeted to special students.

Children With Children

Rather than allow them to drop out, the Austin (Texas) school system established a Teenage Parent Program to give pregnant students the support and eduction they need. It has grown in 13 years from a half-day tutoring program in a local church building to a full-day school in one wing of Allan Elementary School, complete with a well-staffed infant care center.

The halls at Allan look like the halls of any other school. But here, between classes, the students gather not to talk about whom to date or what outfit to wear Friday night, but about doctors' appointments, diaper rash, baby formulas and breast feeding.

The students, who do not want to stay on their home campuses, take a full course load at Allan so that they won't be too far behind when they return to their regular schools. Students must also take a class in child development or independent family living. The average length of stay at Allan is one semester, and before each girl is dismissed, officials make sure adequate child care has been arranged.

Speaking the Unspeakable

Communities today are facing the growing phenomenon of teenage suicide. It's another one of those taboo subjects we never used to talk about, but it has finally gotten the national attention it deserves. And many educators are convinced that the key to stemming the rising tide of young suicides—the number has tripled in the last 25 years—may be the classroom teacher.

One of the most successful suicide-prevention programs in the nation is in the Fairfax County (Va.) Public Schools, where volunteer mental health professionals train every high school and intermediate school teacher in the causes and symptoms of suicide. The program includes seminars for students and also invites parents to attend special PTA meetings with mental health professionals to discuss adolescents' stress-related problems. The use of volunteers keeps the cost down.

Specially trained counselors work with the students to help them cope with those factors that are common to many suicide victims. These include divorced parents, a learning disability, intense academic pressures and a history of moving to many different cities. But they depend on the teachers to be able to identify the troubled youngsters. Teachers deal with students regularly and in smaller numbers than counselors, and are much more likely to detect signs of mental stress.

Schools are the last line of defense for many of these students, because so often at home there is a breakdown in communication. And the teachers feel the seminars they attend have been very helpful in alerting them to signs of depression in their students. Those signs include:

□ Rapid weight loss or gain,
□ Changes in sleep patterns, insomnia or hypersomnia,
□ Loss of interest in usually pleasurable activities,
□ Diminishing ability to think or concentrate,
□ Fatigue,
□ Sense of worthlessness, hopelessness or excessive guilt,
□ Uncharacteristic agitation and hostility and
□ Frank thoughts on suicide, saying such things as "I wish I were dead."

Building Self-Awareness

I'm O.K., You're O.K. is more than the title of a book at Bayshore Elementary School in North Fort Myers, Fla. It's an expression of the kinds of feelings that almost any child in the school is prepared to discuss as the result of a homegrown program of exploring self-awareness.

There was little question such a program was needed at the school, which has one of the highest ratios of minority students in Lee County. Half of the 525 students qualify for free or reduced-price lunches. Counselor Betty Lewis said that 40 percent live in a home with only one of their natural parents. The students took a 58-question yes-or-no self-esteem inventory last year, and as expected, the results demonstrated that the children had very low opinions of themselves.

As a result, the school developed a program to help improve the self-concepts the children had. Here's how the Bayshore program works: Each morning for 15 minutes, the entire school concentrates on student self-awareness. In every classroom, the children discuss their feelings and emotions or express themselves through such outlets as puppetry, self-portraits, flags of their heritage and games. In every classroom and throughout the hallways, visitors can see posters proclaiming "We Can," "I Can," "I Am," and "I'm Glad To Be Me." Students also discuss their Very Important Person Club and what it means to them.

While faculty members are excited about the program's potential, school officials say it is obvious that pupils and their parents are even more so. Parents are excited because they seem to know intuitively what researchers have concluded: what young children think about themselves will affect their future behavior and ability to succeed academically.

CHAPTER SIX

Involving Your Key Publics

Good public relations has always been the art of identifying key publics, and establishing workable mechanisms for informing, listening and involving them with a goal of improving the institution and its services.

For the sake of good public relations—which leads to better education—every school system should build and maintain the best possible support for its schools and the school program.

A positive climate contributes to the total morale of the student body, staff and community. The effort you make to reach all of the people in and around your school community (not just parents) helps build a total positive attitude toward the school system in particular and education in general.

There are countless ways in which a school system can communicate with its many publics. But, it's critical to determine with whom you're communicating when deciding how.

Different publics have different information needs. For the growing audience of adults in the U.S. without children, there may be little information at all, except what they read or hear from the news media. This is especially important when you consider that public education today operates in a fish bowl. Educators in school systems throughout the country are being asked to account for all their actions, including the money spent and the product produced.

In light of what the polls say about public awareness of school programs, educators obviously haven't succeeded in their efforts to inform. And despite the trend toward citizen advisory committees, community participation and other involvement techniques, there are also numerous indicators that educators haven't even been listening.

The wise school district plans a structured communications program to counteract the vagaries of the community's day-to-day contact with its public schools.

Involving Special Publics

While educators have traditionally maintained that schools belong to the public, besides working with the news media (and not always very effectively), most external PR efforts have been focused on parents. Certainly parents are a key public which must be continually informed and involved.

But as the decade of the '80s rolled around, statistics indicated that two-thirds to three-fourths of the adult population no longer have children in schools. And the trend won't reverse significantly in the foreseeable future. In fact, when the decade of the '90s begins, statistics show that there will be more senior citizens in America than children of school age.

What this means is that those who control elections, pay most of the taxes, shape public opinion, and in general control public education, no longer have a stake or personal interest in the form of a child in the public schools. And just as important, these same special publics have the means and the ability, if so motivated, to provide the needed support, additional resources, and learning opportunities for students that schools couldn't buy even if they had the money.

This shift in demographics has tremendous public relations implications for educators—not only in terms of their communication targets, but particularly their communication approaches. News media, the old standby of PR efforts, are still as important as ever since newspapers and broadcast media continue to be the source of information for this new majority audience. But that's as far as it goes. You can't send them your newsletters with the kids, and you can't expect them to come to PTA meetings or open houses.

New and creative efforts will be required if educators are going to reach this critical group. We've got to establish and maintain new friendships—before we need them.

Non-Parents

In NSPRA's book, *Non-Parents and the Schools: Creating a New Team,* Jeanne Magmer, director, public information, Oregon School Boards Assn., writes that "non-parent" groups are by far the largest percentage of taxpayers in any school district. By 1990, the U.S. Census Bureau projects the number of people age 55 and over will be larger than the entire K-12 school population. And, if present trends continue, one out of every five Americans will be at least 55 by the turn of the century.

Education pollster Ned S. Hubbell, director, Project Outreach, Michigan Dept. of Education, also notes in the book that there is a growing information gap between the public schools and the majority of the public. The reason parents feel knowledgeable about schools, and non-parents feel just the opposite, is due to their sources of information.

For parents, the number one source of information is their children, "and that hasn't changed in eight years," Hubbell points out. Next, they rely on the mass media and this is "up significantly . . ." The third source is teachers and other employees; fourth, word-of-mouth from other people; and fifth, school district publications.

For non-parents, the mass media continue to be the primary source, with other sources being word-of-mouth from other people, someone's children, school district publications, and teachers and other school employees.

What people want to know from their schools shows that parents and non-parents share the same mutual information needs and interests.

☐ What's being taught and learned in schools is the number one area of interest. This includes curriculum content priorities and emphasis, especially in basic skills; more about student progress, test results and proof of results. A special interest is in information about curriculum from the secondary schools.

☐ How basic subjects are taught—especially in reading instructions and math skills—includes a need for information about teaching methods, techniques, etc.

☐ How school funds are spent covers budget priorities and the determination of those priorities. Hubbell's studies show that one out of every five adults gives the schools a "poor" rating in informing citizens about financial matters.

☐ How the school board operates and reaches decisions is a new area of interest. Citizens want to know how the board arrives at policies and what procedures are used. Very few people really understand the role, powers, duties and limitations of local boards.

The news media, which, as Hubbell shows, more and more of our publics are depending on for information about schools, carry information about these topics critically or not at all. But, if you look closely at this coverage, you will find they do so more often from lack of information from school administrators than from lack of space or interest from readers.

A bright spot in the research, however, is that nearly three out of every 10 Americans are currently involved in educational activities, and 27% of the population is engaged in providing educational services of one kind or another.

Steps to Identifying Non-Parents

To begin to involve non-parents, Magmer says, you first need to define the term. If by non-parent you mean residents of your district who have no children or who no longer have children in school, your definition is correct but too broad to concentrate your communications efforts effectively.

What you should do, she says, is list specific non-parent publics you want to reach (e.g., senior citizens, business people, young marrieds, single adults, career people, pre-school parents).

Now break each of these publics into target groups. For example, under senior citizens you might list:

- ☐ Residents whose children are grown but continue to live in their homes in your district,
- ☐ Grandparents of the children in your school,
- ☐ Senior citizens at the local community center,
- ☐ Residents who live in one or several condominium developments in your district and
- ☐ Senior citizens confined to full-time care facilities.

Or,

- ☐ Active senior citizens (55 years plus) interested in volunteering in the schools.

Senior Citizens

Our population is steadily growing older. Each day 5,000 U.S. citizens celebrate their 65th birthdays; 25 million people are more than 65 years old.

These older citizens are an invaluable resource for schools. Senior citizens, retired people who have a lot of time and skills, can do everything from tutoring to making learning materials for classroom use. Many have interesting former careers, hobbies, travel experiences, or have lived through interesting historical periods and could share those experiences with students. And all are asked to support schools at the polls.

Unfortunately, senior citizens often have little chance to use their time and skills constructively. They rarely receive information from the schools. So they grow more and more alienated and those school districts that rely on voters for operating funds know exactly what this can mean.

But the senior citizen need not be an adversary of the schools. He or she can be a friend and a key communicator in the community with a little help and recognition from school personnel.

Consequently, schools, if they are to inform older citizens about their programs, problems and needs, can capitalize on the research by bringing older citizens into the schools as volunteers. Being a volunteer is an important service to their communities and can offer opportunities for lifelong learning and enrichment.

Harbor Springs, Mich., is the site of one of the nation's first public schools to try an intergenerational program. The question in 1980 was whether the town should build an expensive islolated center for the area's 400 retired senior citizens or use an existing multi-million-dollar complex staffed by professionals—namely Harbor Springs High School.

A first floor library was converted into the senior citizen friendship center and it didn't take long for the youngsters to find their way there as well. It may have been the free cookies, or competitive Scrabble and cribbage matches, or just someone to talk to. Soon, one of the ladies from the center found her way into a home economic class, where she helps teach embroidery to seventh graders. Elsewhere in the school, a former journalism teacher, who had to retire because of arthritis, helps in the yearbook and journalism class. A blind woman, who is 79, helps a senior who started losing his sight at 13.

The Prairie Norton Elementary School in Columbus, Ohio, has a grandparent program which is a cooperative venture between the school and local senior citizens. Schools are finding that the designation "grand-

Getting Seniors Involved

There are many things senior citizens can do for the schools. And there are many things schools can do for senior citizens. For instance, schools can:

- Seek out and speak with senior citizen groups, urging their members to become school volunteers.
- Provide senior citizens with space for an activities center in a school in which enrollment has declined.
- Provide a special day to recognize and honor senior citizens.
- Issue a courtesy pass—a "Golden Age Card" as some school districts call it—for free admissions to school-sponsored events, such as athletic contests, plays and continuing education classes.
- Provide breakfasts or lunches in school buildings.
- Arrange for use of school buses during non-school hours to take senior citizens to activities of interest to them.
- Appoint a school district staff member to act as liaison with senior citizen groups to keep open lines of communication.
- Invite senior citizens to use school libraries, gyms, swimming pools and other facilities.

parent" is one to which senior citizens do not appear to object. In fact, as one grandmother put it, "We care—just as much as parents do—sometimes more."

How To Start a Program

If a school district wants to start a program involving senior citizens NSPRA offers these tips:

1. A news release can be sent to local papers and carried in district publications telling of the board of education's action to establish a Golden Age Program. Residents of the school district who are 65 years (55 in many programs) or older are asked to call the school information office and request their cards. (Districts having a decentralized program might ask them to call the local elementary school—but, still, a master list should be maintained in the central office.) No credentials are required—take their word.

2. Once a name is received a welcome letter is sent from the superintendent on behalf of the board of education, along with the Golden Age Card for the current year. (This process must be done annually because of deaths, moving, etc.)

3. Along with the letter, enclose a calendar of school events for the year, as well as information about what they may do with the Golden Age Card:
   □ Attend all district athletic, musical and dramatic offerings free of charge.
   □ Attend classes in the Adult Evening School (or Community School) free of charge except for materials used in specific courses.
   □ Indicate they will be invited to other activities during the year by local school principals.

4. After lists are compiled, send them to all school principals along with suggestions for ways they can involve senior citizens in activities, such as:
   □ Aides—reading to students, sharing hobbies such as knitting, woodworking, slides from travels, etc.
   □ Hold special Grandparents Days or Golden Age Days.
   □ Have special events during American Education Week.
   □ Hold a special tea or invite Golden Agers to lunch at school and tour the building.

5. During winter holidays when many of the schools are having programs—send another letter inviting them to these special events and pointing out others that will be coming up.

6. If your state legislature is working on bills that will bring tax relief to senior citizens, encourage the board of education to take some

definite action on the bill, to write letters to their legislators. (Send names and addresses of legislators to your senior citizens.)

7. Put them on lists for all district publications. They may be particularly interested in information for parents of preschool children. Many are grandparents and love hearing about this!

Volunteers

A generation ago, the term volunteer meant *parent* volunteer. But today there are hundreds of other possibilities. They include parents, former teachers, high school students, senior citizens, service clubs, youth organizations, higher education, military installations, women's clubs and fraternal organizations.

And every volunteer a school district can bring in not only helps the schools, but he or she also becomes a goodwill ambassador.

According to school district reports, the widespread use of volunteers can have these beneficial results (among others):

□ Volunteers save money for the schools and give students more individual attention.

□ They free teachers and staff from some of the necessary paperwork.

□ Volunteers in the classroom usually result in fewer discipline problems because there is adult supervision.

□ Volunteers become a link between the school and the community.

Experience, however, has taught many districts that certain cautions must be observed and certain guidelines must be followed.

□ Staff members often need to be "sold" on the contribution that volunteers can make.

□ The program requires an effective training program for the volunteers.

□ The volunteer program must be coordinated and supervised by someone.

□ Someone in each school must be responsible for welcoming and supervising volunteers.

□ Volunteers should be given work that is challenging and interesting—their jobs shouldn't be dull and tedious.

It is extremely important to recognize the work done by volunteers and to genuinely pat them on the back now and then. Saying "Thank you," or showing appreciation for the help schools receive from volunteers is essential. It also is a good way to find out how well you are doing.

In the Everett (Wash.) school district, for example, the PTA sponsors an annual "Golden Acorn Award." Each school attendance area gives a Golden Acorn Award pin to a citizen of the area whose service to schools has been "above and beyond the call of duty."

Volunteers and Children with Special Needs

Many school volunteers today are working with children who have special learning needs. In its book on *Volunteers and Children with Special Needs,* the National School Volunteer Program, Inc., (NSVP) notes that many children who are not succeeding in school can become achievers if they get extra help and drill which is designed to meet their individual learning needs. "They will benefit most from such extra help if it is given on a one-to-one basis or in a small group," the NSVP says. "Volunteers can help busy teachers to supply this extra attention and reinforcement to learning."

According to the NSVP, although volunteers often create learning games and activities, it is the teacher's role to diagnose learning problems and prescribe strategies and activities to meet each child's needs. The teacher also gives the volunteer information about children's strengths and weaknesses and explains classroom routines and procedures, materials, holidays and field trips. Most important is the teacher's ability to make the volunteer feel comfortable as part of the education team.

Churches

Still another key public is the community's churches.

Schools should recognize the influence that churches represent within the community and decide on a course of action for better communication between two strong institutions. Ask the clergy for their concerns and their recommendations for strengthening communications—and building public confidence in the schools.

For several years, the Dallas (Texas) public schools have sponsored a special "Education Sunday" during American Education Week to highlight the importance of public education in society. Judicatory heads in the Dallas area have endorsed the observance and the concept of reconnecting the school and the churches.

"Certainly reasoning power, intellectual attainment, the development of leadership skills and character building are among the goals which our religious and educational institutions share," Bobbie Foster, director of community relations for the Dallas (Texas) school system, says.

"Schools and churches have always played a key role in the education and molding of youth. Since these two institutions also play such an important part in the quality of life in any community, the need to work together is readily apparent," Foster points out.

During "Education Sunday" in Dallas, special information is sent to churches to be included in church bulletins and Dallas educators are available to attend Sunday services and conduct informal discussions about education with the congregation. Printed materials about the school district are available to interested participants.

The school district also has established a Religious Community Task Force. Members include representatives from the Interdenominational Ministerial Alliance, the Dallas Religious Judicatories, the Dallas Pastors Association, the Rabbinical Association, the Companerismo Ecumenico Pastoral, Church Women United and the Greater Dallas Community of Churches.

"What we tried to do is develop more trust and better communications between the schools and various sectors of the citizenry," said a spokesman for the task force. Strong support and continuous information was fed into the school district and numerous activities began. High school "clusters" set up lines of communication through church volunteers; a Community Forum on Public Education was co-sponsored by religious leadership; church bulletin inserts and pulpit announcements "spread the word" about education; and Block Partnership staffs were assigned to assist the school staff in its community work.

The positive efforts of ministers, priests and rabbis across the city, in rich and poor congregations, in all ethnic communities, in every neighborhood—all this has led to more than 100 school "adoptions" by area churches, a sense of access to the schools through familiar and trusted persons, and many more community resources for the public schools.

Selling Realtors on Your Schools

The interdependence between schools and real estate is not a new phenomenon. For years, the traditional approach to buying one's home was to locate a chosen school and then find available housing nearby.

"What about the schools?" is second only to price on the list of questions clients usually ask their realtor. Yet, it is often a question many real estate agents are least equipped to answer.

Times have changed many circumstances surrounding the distance between home and school, but nothing has altered the vital link between the public's perception of a city's schools and city's housing values.

Add to a realtor's lack of knowledge any school-related controversy—a court-ordered desegregation plan for instance—and you've got a salesperson who's likely to recommend the local non-public schools or a nearby district, says John T. Holton, supervisor of information services for the Red Clay Consolidated School District in Wilmington, Del.

"Such was the case in New Castle County, Del., where the realtors, wary of dealing with the 'busing' issue, simply pushed homes in surrounding areas or told the buyers to take the house but opt for non-public schools," Holton said. "But that situation ignored two truths: that the public schools had rebounded well from the initial setback accompanying desegregation and that there was a real estate boom begging to happen in that area. Today, the schools and the realtors are partners in a community where schools and housing are growth markets."

Tip Sheet Working With Realtors

☐ At school opening time hold a forum for a panel of school officials and an audience of realtors to talk about schools—changes to be aware of, bringing new realtors up to speed and generally rekindling the cooperative spirit.

☐ Hold a Realtor's Dinner featuring education as its theme—student groups perform, student work is displayed, and the keynote address is by an educator.

☐ Throughout the year, on a rotating basis, schools can host realtor tours—sales people from all firms serving the school's community get a briefing from the principal, visit classrooms in action and talk to parents and students.

☐ Print a "whom to call" directory of the district for each realtor based on the questions they are most frequently asked.

☐ A brochure, "The ABC's of Public Education," helps realtors answer client's initial questions about schools.

In addition, Sally Keeler, community relations coordinator for the Montgomery County (Md.) Public Schools suggests getting the local board of realtors to alert its members when you have new publications available, with a reminder every few months. Ask to put a note in the newsletter with your phone number. Keep realtors on your mailing lists. Make certain they have early notification (before they read it in the newspaper) of any changes in school boundary lines or planned school closings. Some school systems go so far as to print and revise annually a special "Realtor's Notebook" containing school boundary maps, names of local school officials and facts and figures about the school district budget, operation, etc.

New Residents

When a family with children moves into a new area, one of their first concerns is the schools. And here, perhaps more than anywhere else, first impressions last a long, long time.

What is the first impression a family gets of a school district? A curt secretary or receptionist at the central office who has had a rough day and really doesn't feel like being a public relations persons, too? A school official who doesn't have time to answer a lot of questions? A principal who's constantly "in conference?" A teacher-neighbor who doesn't hesitate to knock the school district?

Faced with these possibilities, if not realities, many school districts gear a public relations program directly toward new residents registering their children in the school district for the first time. One of these is the Central Bucks School District in suburban Philadelphia, Pa. These efforts are what school officials call the "personal touch."

When new residents come to the central administration building to determine where their children will be assigned or to gather information about the school district, the receptionist is friendly and accommodating. She encourages them to help themselves to school publications. Even those who come without appointments are usually ushered into the community relations office immediately where their questions are answered and specific materials are identified which pertain to the school their children will attend. They are given a map and directions to their new school.

High school students are particularly apprehensive about changing to a new school, so the school district has school newspapers, course guides and sports schedules available for parents to take along. If the students come too, the district suggests that they go to their new school where they can meet the counselors and look around.

The school visit can be a shocking experience if the first thing the secretary does there is to thrust a fist full of forms at them and tells them to fill them out. The school districts suggest that principals meet the new parents, answer their questions, take them on a tour of the school, and ask about the kind of program and school the children are coming from. That helps the parents feel more welcome, while it gives the school principal or counselors some insights into the new children who, although they are strangers, must be matched up with teachers and class assignments.

Often new residents call the district office to determine which schools their children will attend and how to go about registering them. These persons are referred directly to the schools and sent materials about the district. The school principal also is asked to send them a welcoming letter and registration forms so that they can be completed before the first visit.

The school system's cardinal rule is to receive people warmly and try to avoid as much red tape as possible.

Business and Industry

Another key area of communication is business and industry. Efforts to aid appear to be on the rise. The business community should and usually does feel a commitment to the schools. Business can interact with schools by providing opportunities for field trips; by serving as role models in apprenticeship programs; by serving as members of advisory committees; by providing released time for employees to work as school volunteers; by supporting organizations in the school; by serving as community resource volunteers; by giving presentations for career education or general interest subjects; by adopting a school or a program and by providing personnel and resources to support the school.

In Dallas, Texas, more than 400 companies are providing up to $3 million in cash, services and materials to more than 200 public schools annually. The Adopt-A-School program has grown from 13 businesses, 15 religious groups and six organizations 10 years ago to 2,153 adopting groups in 1985.

In Philadelphia, Pa., industry established an electrical academy in one high school, a business academy in another, and an aviation academy in a third, providing both equipment for the academies and expertise in setting them up.

In Memphis, Tenn., the Federal Express Company raised $1 million to build an addition to a school for the handicapped. In Los Angeles, Calif., employees of about 105 firms help out in 115 schools. Copying its New York City program, Mobil Corporation will contribute more than $600,000 over three years to bring performing artists into the schools of Washington, D.C.

In these types of cooperative arrangements, the schools gain help and encouragement from business, and these volunteers gain new insights into the schools. And although such arrangements began in the large cities, cooperative ventures with business and industry are important in smaller school districts, too, particularly in light of the rising tax burden borne by businesses for local schools.

Principals and superintendents should make it their business to seek out and communicate with local chambers of commerce and service clubs composed primarily of businesspeople.

School Partnerships

Four years ago, the Atlanta (Ga.) city school system went to the local business community with a proposition. "Join us as working partners in the educational process," asked the schools, "and we will upgrade the quality of education in a system that otherwise faces some big economic and social problems."

The promised payoff to the local business community would be a school system with employable graduates, and a system strong enough to help attract new investments to Atlanta. The result of that meeting between top school officials and senior executives of some 200 Atlanta corporations was the creation of **Atlanta Partnership of Business and Education, Inc.,** a non-profit organization that has since attracted national attention.

"We felt when we began that we could promise the business leaders a return on their investment," said Boyd D. Odom, executive director of the Atlanta Partnership.

That "return" might be expressed in several ways, according to Odom:

- □ A city with a strong school system attracts new business and industry.
- □ A community with employable public school graduates has lower welfare and poverty rates.
- □ Businesses prosper when their employees have job skills. Specifically, the executives were told that a successful partnership between business and public schools would contribute to a lower student drop-out rate, improved attendance, upgraded scholastic performance and in the community-at-large, a reduced crime rate.

A partnership was established slowly at first with fewer than 70 business firms and organizations. But today it includes the active participation of over 200 business firms.

The total dollar value of that contribution has roughly doubled each year since 1981 when the program was established. During the 1985 school year business firms will contribute support valued at $4 million, said Odom, calling it a conservative estimate.

Has the Atlanta Partnership been effective? Odom insists that the organization cannot claim credit for all that has happened in Atlanta's school system since 1981, but he points out that "all the things we said would happen have happened!"

- □ Average daily attendance in the city schools has improved from 90 percent in 1980 to 93 percent in 1984.
- □ The drop-out rate fell from 5.9 percent to 4 percent, and was projected to fall below that in 1985.
- □ Scholastic performance, as measured by standardized reading and math test scores, improved dramatically.

□ The Atlanta Police Department crime rate figures improved from a total monthly average of 5,584 in 1980 to 4,197 in the first half of 1984.

How To Get Started

Business leaders are anxious to work with schools, but many feel that educators do not seem to want them. Invite leaders in your area to visit the school district and discuss ways you can work together. Share your needs and ask that they join you in seeking solutions. Businesspeople are concerned that too often educators ask for financial support, but do not welcome involvement. Businesspeople, already heavily involved financially through taxation, will frequently be willing to provide people, facilities and opportunities for training students and staff members.

Here's what Rockwell International official Ray Reed of Dallas, Texas, says about his company's involvement with the schools:

"We won't bite. Come to us and ask us for help. We are open, are receptive to whatever schools would like us to do. We want this to be a cooperative effort. We are not trying to infringe on their turf, and we realize the educator has his or her responsibility and they are working hard to implant knowledge and to educate our children. We also feel that we have an equal responsibility to help in this endeavor. We don't want them to feel shy, and afraid of asking us for assistance because we are ready, willing and able to provide that assistance. I know it will work, because if it doesn't work, we are in trouble. We are in trouble from the standpoint of the future of our country, and I am most concerned about the future of our country. And as you know, the future of our country lies in the hands of our young people, and if business, industry, the school district and all other entities in the community don't work together, our nation is not going to be as strong as it should be and can be."

Adopt-A-School

Put your school up for "adoption." The Adopt-A-School movement is growing in schools and districts across the nation. A business, civic or community group can help a school meet many of its needs with volunteers, sponsorship of activities, funding of equipment or materials, even instructors in special programs.

Business-school partnerships not only increase education opportunities for students, but promote the community and its schools as an attraction for industrial growth.

□ Develop a speakers bureau of business leaders in the community willing to serve as classroom speakers to discuss careers and training.

- [ ] Volunteer your services and the services of teachers and students to work with local businesses as a presentation team to recruit new business and industry for your school community.
- [ ] Invite business leaders to assist with programs for the gifted and talented, as well as vocational-technical students; to serve as guest lecturers in science, mathematics, engineering and other areas; to offer special programs in their companies and serve as role models for students.

Business-School Involvement

In an *Education USA* Special Report on *Business-School Partnerships: A Plus For Kids,* Richard Lesher's five characteristics of businessmen and women that educators may overlook are listed. Lesher, president of the U.S. Chamber of Commerce says:

1. Businessmen and women are former students.
2. Most are parents and grandparents and as such are interested in how well schools are educating their children and grandchildren.
3. They're major employers . . . more than four out of five jobs are still in the private sector.
4. They are management experts who can help educators manage their limited resources more efficiently.
5. And, they are community-minded leaders.

A sixth point Lesher should have added is that business is a microcosm of the community as a whole. The ratio of parents to non-parents in business is as high as it is in the community. The misinformation businesspeople have about education is colored not only by the kinds of things they learn from the mass media and hear from their neighbors and friends, but also by the kinds of applicants public schools send through their doors.

The *Education USA* Special Report lists four kinds of business-industry involvement with schools taking place throughout the country.

- [ ] **Collaborative activities** which directly or indirectly involve students. These usually are career preparation or awareness programs, or in economic or citizenship education.
- [ ] **Cooperative efforts** to aid schools or school districts that don't involve students. Examples include management studies, staff development, teachers in industry programs, budget preparation assistance, long-range planning.
- [ ] **Involvement** by individuals from business and industry as members of boards, committees or task forces.
- [ ] **Education**-related activities by business or industry without the cooperation of local schools or school districts.

Programs under the first three kinds of involvement above are especially helpful to a district's communications efforts with the larger community. School districts are finding, too, business is more than willing to be involved with schools. All that's needed is for someone to ask them.

CHAPTER SEVEN

Managing Critical Issues

One thing is certain. All school systems have critical problems. There are hundreds, perhaps thousands of different kinds, and they vary in size and intensity. But they are definitely there. And the school district that pretends they aren't is in trouble with its community already.

That is why all school districts should have detailed public relations plans not only for communicating problems frankly and objectively to the community, but for telling the community, forthrightly, what they are doing about them, and, perhaps most critically, for identifying them before they become a problem.

Such a procedure instills public confidence and support. The lack of such a procedure invites public scorn and non-support.

Issues Management

One of the newest management tools in school public relations is that of **issues management.** It does not replace a strong, ongoing and effective public relations program, but it does allow school PR professionals to fine tune their programs and manage the future more effectively.

Donald L. Ferguson, vice president, Intercom, Inc., and editor of *Scanner*, the issues management newsletter published by NSPRA, believes the role of an effective issues manager must go beyond merely being able to identify and manage current "hot issues" or problems. "The effective issues manager, regardless of what industry, must respond to the challenge of adequately preparing to handle those issues that are emerging or are virtually impossible to predict," he says. "And more importantly, the issues manager, PR specialist or school administrator must be able to respond in a timely, positive and proactive manner."

Schools face hundreds of issues. Special interest groups place continual demands on educators and boards. Schools generally respond by being

reactive; mitigating the impact on school programs and budgets if possible; adopting positive changes where practical.

Some school districts in the country have moved to develop an issues management program designed to help their school system become **proactive** in identifying, managing, and resolving major issues they face. While a growing number of Fortune 500 companies conduct such activities, true issues management is only starting to develop in the field of education.

Several intermediate school districts—most notably Macomb in Michigan—have initiated systems of issues management. A few state education agencies have explored the concept including Alaska. The San Diego (Calif.) County School System is using the system to set the agenda for the future. San Diego staff members have started to determine what they want to happen in education, in their community and in the legislative arena. Then, they will put their efforts behind shaping the desired future.

An early adapter of issues management was Larry Ascough, special assistant to the superintendent in the Dallas (Texas) Independent School District, who began developing a system in 1983.

The Dallas PR staff had been informally monitoring and analyzing issues on a day-to-day basis for a number of years. But after watching the issues management field grow, the Dallas staff decided it was time to formalize its efforts.

The first step (as it should be in any system) was agreeing on the definition of an issue. In the Dallas system it's defined as a "trend or condition, internal or external, which may, will, or does have an effect on the successful accomplishment of objectives." In the school business that can be a long list, and the Dallas team identified more than 200 issues at the outset.

As the Dallas staff agreed, issues management is really a simple concept: identifying trends . . . prioritizing them in accordance with interests and resources . . . developing a plan of action . . . and following through. Basically, it's common sense, and it's easy to do with the aid of modern technology.

The Dallas team was already aware of the value of monitoring issues. It soon discovered that with a little work and creativity, plus technology, it was possible to track several hundred at one time; manage priorities, be prepared to mount immediate efforts for emerging issues when they reached specific levels, and keep management informed on a variety of issues at all times.

Like any workable system, there had to be guidelines. So the staff developed a set of procedures divided into 12 major issue categories based on the district's organizational structure. An ongoing identification process, involving employees at all levels, was designed to feed the system with potential issues.

An Issues Management Task Force, composed of the superintendent and the top staff, reviews the potential issues on a bi-weekly basis. The group sets priorities on possible issues, reviews the status of issues already in the system and monitors the progress of issues strategies. Here's the route of an issue through the system:

1. It is identified as a potential issue.
2. It is referred to the task force for consideration.
3. It is sent to the appropriate staff liaison person (called a **"key link"** in the DISD) who represents one of the 12 issue categories.
4. The liaison person identifies the best available expert who drafts a recommended **position paper** (based on a brief standard format).
5. The draft is reviewed by the appropriate department head and returned to the task force.
6. The task force accepts, rejects or asks for modifications in the paper.
7. The paper becomes part of the **electronic monitoring system.**

The preceding is obviously over-simplified, but basically that's how it works, Ascough says. The key issues management players include:

☐ The liaisons (links) who keep the issues papers updated;
☐ The experts who draft papers, maintain related files and develop strategies;
☐ The system manager (the PR person) who oversees the operation;
☐ The system operator who inputs and maintains the software program; and
☐ The issues management task force.

The Dallas system has listed seven major accomplishments in its initial years:

1. The electronic anticipation and tracking system is in place.
2. Management is "forced" to deal with issues by the system.
3. A "common" position has been developed on key issues.
4. Staff has a "party line" to follow on key issues.
5. Files on key issues are readily available.
6. Issues that may have otherwise gone ignored are being addressed.
7. A true "bottoms up" opportunity exists for staff.

Thus this new approach of issues management provides school administrators, staff and public relations specialists with a needed method of improving a school district's public relations plan of action. The tracking process enables a district to evaluate problems emerging across the nation and prepare in advance to meet the challenges.

Impact of the "New Right"

Such an issue is that of the activities of the New Right, which could result in reaffirming the values that keep the country together, but if unchecked, could destroy them, according to J. Charles Park, professor

of education at the University of Wisconsin at Whitewater, a key re-
searcher on the New Right.

Park urges school officials to educate their staffs and communities
about democracy in education. He says they should "campaign more
vigorously for democratic schools than the New Right groups campaign
against the public schools."

Park says school systems which do not have procedures for dealing
with controversies are in trouble now. He urges educators to study their
communities with great care, analyzing the psychology of their alienated
groups; and practice being in a conflict situation.

The New Right is not just a conservative political faction—although it
clearly is that. The movement is also highly religion-based, so that its
members feel comfortable that they are acting in accordance with God's
will. The New Right does not deal only with national issues. The movement also is a grassroots effort, working to influence state legislatures,
parents, state departments of education and local school boards, according to Park.

In NSPRA's book, *New Voices on the Right: Impact on Schools,* Joseph
P. Rowson, former administrative assistant for publications/information
in the Lincoln (Neb.) Public Schools, now director of public affairs,
University of Nebraska, says it is clear that those who work in school
systems—particularly public school systems—are quite likely to encounter the New Right. And, it is likely, too, that the encounter will be a
negative one, sparked by complaints.

"Even if school teachers, administrators or board members agree in
principle with causes of the New Right, they are likely to come under fire
if they attempt to avoid censorship or refuse to breach the law of the land
by imposing a particular religious viewpoint on students," Rowson writes.
"The very defense of society's 'secular laws,' which offend 'God's laws'
is cause for approbation by the New Right."

Censorship

From the educator's viewpoint, the most important single issue posed
by the new political/religious movement on the right is that of censorship.
It is the single most pervasive concern because it affects practically all
parts of the country and because it can restrict the materials classroom
teachers use to teach, the books available to students in their libraries
and the curriculum in our schools.

How can school board members, school administrators, and the public
relations people who serve school systems and concerned parents and
community leaders meet the challenges posed?

Barbara Kudlacek, public relations director for the Topeka (Kan.) Public Schools, says before any formal challenges have been filed, but when information on school programs has been sought by groups, the school systems should take the following steps:

- ☐ Meet with leaders of the teachers' association and with the media center or library staff to review policies and procedures and to make sure a workable process is in place.
- ☐ Meet with school principals to review what to do if someone shows up wanting to review materials or to sit in on a class.
- ☐ Discuss the issue with the management of news media and with education reporters, pointing out that both the schools and the news media are the focus of attack by any group seeking **censorship.**
- ☐ Provide information about the group and its activities as background information for board of education members.

After the New Right group has "gone public" and is making clear its intention to change school programs, Kudlacek says the following steps should be followed:

- ☐ Monitor the group's public meetings to help identify issues.
- ☐ Discuss the issues with teacher groups to allay fears that teachers would receive no support from the administration if their materials or instruction are challenged.
- ☐ Arrange for supporters of current school programs under attack to speak at the same board meeting as leaders of the attacking group.
- ☐ Focus on programs under attack in staff and community newsletters, so people are well informed about the program and its instructional value.
- ☐ Provide background information for news media, being careful to give objective information on both sides of the issue.
- ☐ Meet with the local religious council or ministerial alliance to discuss programs under attack, setting a follow-up detailed workshop on each program for those who desire more information and want to talk to instructors or library people involved.

Gary Marx, associate executive director for the American Association of School Administrators (AASA), believes that school systems can effectively handle the challenges posed by the New Right and other types of pressure groups. The steps he recommends:

- ☐ Accept the fact that dissent is part of our system.
- ☐ Conduct regular formal or informal opinion polls to determine community feelings on various issues.
- ☐ Adopt policies which assure community involvement.
- ☐ Work effectively with advisory groups.
- ☐ Develop programs and plans that represent the greatest degree of community consensus while insuring the best education possible for kids.

- [ ] Be sure those programs and plans are understood by board members, staff and community.
- [ ] Make your decision, but continue to listen. Make allowances for those valid concerns and ideas missed in the initial process.

Legislation for Schools

As school districts identify critical issues, they need to identify those critical legislative issues effecting education and become actively involved with the decision makers at their state capitals.

Gone are the days when school districts could, and did, leave state politics to the state politicians. It used to be that most schools were funded primarily from local funds, and what went on in smoke-filled rooms at the state capital was of little consequence back home in the local school district.

Lobby for Your Schools

- [ ] Be familiar with the political system in your state and district. Know who is who, how they really feel on issues; who calls the shots; the process of funding; know as much political history as possible.
- [ ] Be able to translate priorities to the funding decision makers, whoever they might be.
- [ ] Identify "friends of education" and seek their advice.

As for politicians:

- [ ] Know them on a first-name basis.
- [ ] Schedule or make frequent visits, but don't bore them.
- [ ] Keep them informed. Make certain that legislators are included on the district's mailing list so they are appraised of school issues. Before the legislative session, invite state legislators in your school district to a breakfast or luncheon get-together with board members and selected administrators. Give them background information on the district, and discuss educational issues relating to legislation. Let them know how it will affect the district.
- [ ] As soon as the legislature convenes, prepare a compact, pocket-sized legislative compendium stating the district's stand on specific bills. Update this regularly as legislation is changed and new bills are introduced. Be sure to list names, titles and phone numbers of administrators

But that is not necessarily the case anymore as state legislatures and state departments of education have more and more to say about federal funds, about special education, and most importantly, about new and complex state school funding formulas. The need for active school district staff efforts are obvious:

☐ More and more states are providing more funds for public education, as local and federal funding gets less and less. Your district should be there to compete with other state services, agencies and school districts for available state dollars.

☐ The basic needs of district schools are best known by the local boards and local administrators. Your district should forward its own legislative proposals to facilitate the operation of schools and to block the passage of legislation which could adversely affect the operation of schools.

☐ Too many education decisions are being made by those who do not

and board members so they can call if there is a question.

☐ Use your publics to communicate agreed-upon needs— letters, visits, forums, editorials, etc.

☐ Have decision makers visit programs in schools. Don't forget to include legislators in other things going on during the course of the school year. Invite them to conferences and discussions, school dedications, budget hearings, etc.

☐ Avoid getting involved in partisan politics.

☐ Avoid philosophical tangles with unions, associations and special interest groups.

☐ Avoid "overkill" in working with legislative decision makers.

☐ Avoid being misunderstood. Be clear, concise, to the point.

☐ Make sure that legislators know and respect their school district source. Your word is your bond. Never promise anything you can't deliver.

☐ Don't claim credit and don't gossip about legislators. If you are crossed politically, don't get angry. Look for friends in unusual places. In politics, a friend is someone who works with you on a particular issue.

☐ Invest in allies and neutral legislators. Don't waste time on opponents who are publicly committed to a position.

have sufficient information to make the proper decisions. Your district should provide current, accurate information quickly to your legislators who need assistance in order to know which way to vote on a bill.

□ Since public education receives its support through and by the political system, it is imperative that the administrator be a part of this system.

A strong lobbying effort can serve to secure adequate funds for the school district; maintain the maximum home rule authority for the school board; protect the school district against adverse legislation; create a statewide education lobby whose voice will be effective in the state capital and advance a substantive legislative program which can enhance the operation of the school district.

Conclude any lobbying effort by issuing a complete report on the final results of the legislative session. Send appropriate "thank you" notes from the school board and superintendent to legislators, education officials, representatives of state associations and other citizens who assisted in any way with the lobbying effort. Assign and distribute copies of all new legislation to the appropriate school officials for review and implementation.

Crisis Planning

Childnapping, bomb threats, tornado alerts, gas explosions, icy weather which causes school closings, an armed robbery, or death or injury at school! No school system is immune to an emergency or disaster having an immediate and negative physical or mental effect on its students, teachers or staff.

Planning for crisis is just one part of planning for a total communications program. Sooner or later you will find yourself in some kind of crisis.

Gayle S. Colley, assistant superintendent, communication information and personnel services, Madison School District #38, Phoenix, Ariz., notes that crisis takes many shapes and is often tragic and unexpected. "With effective pre-planning you will probably survive the crisis well," Colley says.

> "On the other hand, the crisis may be easier to cope with than a damaged reputation if there is ineffective communication. With a plan, you can communicate in a proactive fashion. In a proactive mode the communication is initiated by you, allowing more flexibility and control. Credibility is better with news media and constituents."

Colley says when there is a crisis, school officials should take care of the disaster situation first—protect human welfare and then deal with the communication aspects.

"Credibility is your most valuable asset in a crisis," she says. "An ongoing public relations program based on candid, open communication between the institution and its publics pays great dividends in a crisis. It's essential for every institution to have a written crisis communication plan. Distribute it widely, update it continually, and evaluate it realistically."

Crisis Communication Plan
Richardson (Texas) Public Schools

Determine the Need:

□ Talk with several key communicators (superintendent of schools, supervisors of maintenance, security, building principals at different grade levels, some news media representatives).

□ Explore their perceptions of how they would react to different kinds of crisis situations; listen to the process they would follow and keep a mental tally of the contacts they would make.

□ Discuss your findings with your superintendent and get a decision to follow through.

Gathering Data:

□ Take an open-ended survey of principals and other central staff members to determine topics for crisis plan.

□ Survey specific topics of interest to elementary principals, secondary principals, central administrators.

□ Prepare a matrix of topics most desired.

Writing Your Plan:

□ Form a representative committee, preferably of volunteers, made up of principals, secretaries, parents, central administrators, counselors and students; a geographic distribution in large districts is necessary.

□ Keep your number of meetings and the length of each meeting to a minimum; spread the work load by use of subcommittees and writers for each action plan.

□ Gather data; hold report meetings; keep a firm deadline for submitting action plans.

Select a Format, Print and Distribute:

□ Use a standardized notebook format and action plan design (use colored dividers and paper if possible).

□ Prepare a distribution list seeking input from principals, superintendents, directors, other central administrators.

Similarly, the Parkway (Mo.) School District provides an **Emergency and Disaster Plan Checklist** "to help minimize the risk of major oversights or other errors while operating in the glare of publicity under stress conditions."

The immediate purpose of the plan is to get the facts to families, friends and the general public—and to the proper authorities—as quickly as they are known and as often as new facts become known. The checklist includes the following guidelines:

☐ Immediately notify the appropriate agency or agencies such as police, fire, ambulance, hospital or health authorities.

☐ Insure the safety of all students, staff and other persons in the immediate area.

☐ Refer all news media representatives to the superintendent's office or school-community relations office.

☐ In the event of a major disaster or crisis, a press room will be set up in the district administration center equipped with desks, chairs, typewriters, telephones, etc.

☐ Additional operators will be provided to handle calls coming to the district switchboard.

☐ It is the responsibility of the superintendent's office to notify district attorneys and insurance agents.

Here are some things you should have ready in case of a crisis:

☐ A general description of your institution,

☐ Access to important equipment,

☐ Enough people to handle a large number of inquiries,

☐ Space for news media representatives,

☐ Security personnel,

☐ Extra copies of the crisis communication plan,

☐ Businesses which support schools by advertising in school programs,

☐ Businesses which happen to be within the boundaries of your district,

☐ Businesses which hire high school students,

☐ Businesses in the greater area which send speakers to schools for career education programs.

Start Building Coalitions

For education leaders and their staffs working to manage critical issues no effort is more important than that expended to build coalitions within the community to support quality education.

It's difficult for parents, legislators, and other taxpayers to understand us. Especially when they see us calling each other names during negotiations or strikes, in many states. Television views of teachers throwing rocks at administrators entering buildings during a strike don't build confidence in the schools where those people work. Neither do board comments that teachers aren't doing a good enough job to deserve a decent salary raise.

The point is: we must stop fighting among ourselves and start building coalitions to support quality education. That means teachers, administrators, the business community, the PTAs and anyone else we can identify to build a united front—a coalition—to wake the town and tell the people about education's needs, accomplishments and challenges.

Former AASA President Lloyd Neilsen put it this way:

"The mutual dependence of the world outside of schools and the schools upon the world outside is being recognized by all parties. The effort is being made then, too, on the part of the schools, to respond to this concern of the external groups and at the same time for the external groups to know what the primary needs of the eductional system are."

Coalition-building is not a panacea for public schools, but it can be a powerful, unifying element for them. Typical coalitions include members from teachers organizations, chambers of commerce, parent groups, labor groups, news media, religious organizations and city officials.

Step-by-step guidelines for forming coalitions include selecting an issue, identifying affected groups, calling a meeting, selecting a leader, reaching a consensus on the issue and reaching a consensus on the next step. One of the most important points to remember during any coalition meeting is never to vote on an issue. A coalition should always reach a **consensus.** Voting won't work because it only creates factions.

Superintendent Sandi Terrill of Ell-Saline (Kan.) Unified School District, says several state coalitions of educational organizations have recently been formed. She sent surveys to five educational organizations in each of the 50 states which resulted in the identification of 42 coalitions in existence in 37 states during the 1983-84 school year.

Descriptive data was used to classify these coalitions into four categories based on their degree of formalization and purpose. The overwhelming purpose of these coalitions was to form a united front to address or influence legislative activities. An additional purpose was to improve the public image of education. Improved communication and relationships between member organizations were outcomes of coalition formation.

Coalition operation was most often hindered by labor versus management conflicts and by lack of resources. Top organization leaders represented their organizations in the coalitions with coalition work done by organizational staffs. Administrator, school board, teacher and PTA groups were the most frequent participants in coalitions. All interview respondents considered the coalitions most effective.

Dallas' Coalition, Advocacy Group

Obviously, broad-based community activities on behalf of the public schools would be chaotic without a coordinated effort. The **Community Network for Public Education** in the Dallas (Texas) school system provides the "umbrella" for all groups working to improve the schools.

The Network, as it is commonly called, was formed in early 1976 and continues to operate today. It gives all groups in the school system the opportunity to sit down at a table together, voice concerns and come to a consensus. The original goal of the Network was the peaceful implementation of the Dallas desegregation order through an informed public.

Jim Oberwetter of the Hunt Oil Company was the original chairperson of the Network. "At first, we invited all parties interested in a peaceful implementation of the court order to a series of meetings," he says. "When scores of people showed up representing different constituencies, we felt some kind of structure was needed to provide a framework for the overall effort." The result was the formation of eight task forces representing broad groups within the community.

These task forces are Business, Higher/Private Education, Organization/Agencies, PTA, Realtors, Religious Community, Youth Services and District Advisory Committees. Although task forces and the groups within them might represent differing points of view, all have worked together toward the goal of quality education for the children of Dallas' public schools.

Oberwetter says, "The diversity was an important factor. As a businessman, it was interesting to see how many diverse people, with different interests and concerns, could come to a single goal—peaceful implementation (of the desegregation court order)."

When schools opened without incident in late August 1976, the first goal of the Network had been met. But community leaders and the school district realized the value of maintaining the group's commitment.

The Network still meets on a monthly basis to discuss problems and progress in the schools. Its activities have included support of two successful school bond issues, and an 18-month information campaign to tell citizens about the public school system.

In addition, the Dallas school system is fortunate to have its own advocacy group known as the **Positive Parents of Dallas.** Formed in 1982, the Positive Parents of Dallas is a unique blend of public and private interests that supports Dallas public schools. The organization features the people-power of the PTA and the influence and resources of the Dallas business community.

Through the use of advertising, public relations, and community involvement, the Positive Parents have helped increase student enrollment throughout the Dallas public schools, particularly in neighborhoods where many families traditionally are committed to private education. By showcasing public school excellence, the Positive Parents organization has helped reverse inaccurate perceptions, bring widespread recognition to the Dallas school people and program and inspire renewed commitment to public education.

Dallas Superintendent Linus Wright believes every school system should have such a group. "They have done and can do things we don't or can't," Wright wrote recently. "For example, citizen groups have more credibility since they don't have an obvious self-interest. Often such groups have access to more resources, both human and financial, for use in promoting schools.

"Another is the variety of existing communication channels. There are many natural links in the community which make it possible for advocates to get the word out quickly without reinventing the wheel. Finally, there's effectiveness. Because of the previously mentioned factors, efforts put forth by community groups to help schools communicate are usually more effective than in-house efforts."

Wright offers these tips for school systems interested in developing advocacy groups:

- □ **Conduct a self-examination.** Every school system has traditional supporters: parents, community, business groups and employee organizations. Make a list of current supporters. Analyze your relationship with each; pinpoint strategies for enhancing and expanding coalitions.

- □ **Explore new markets.** Identify groups, institutions, and individuals with whom you share common interests. Pursue the numerous agencies, self-interest groups and even other educational institutions in your community. Agree on appropriate relationships and include them in your network.

- □ **Establish a coordinating mechanism.** Everyone gets involved for a reason. But one thing is for sure. They want to maintain their identity. The secret to juggling diverse groups and interests and moving them toward a common objective is a non-threatening management system. You might consider a neutral, informal coordinating body without official rules or regulations. Make sure everyone has an equal voice and focuses on things which can be accomplished.

- □ **Provide care and feeding.** Getting started is the easy part. The tough job is keeping the effort going. That means providing adequate staff, keeping the channels of communications open, assessing the efforts, making adjustments where necessary and recognizing and rewarding individuals for their efforts.

□ **Suggest ideas and ways others can help.** Make sure you can be specific on how groups and individuals can be of assistance and make sure everyone in the system knows, too. There's nothing worse than asking for help and then not knowing what to do with it when it shows up.

Key Communicators

One of the simplest, and perhaps most often overlooked ways to build support is through networks of those key individual communicators within the community itself.

Donald R. Bagin, professor, communications coordinator, graduate program, school public relations, at Glassboro (N.J.) State College, says key communicators are those people on the school staff and in the community who talk to and are believed by lots of people. When these people are believed and trusted by many others, they become **key communicators.**

Bagin says school officials who identify these key communicators and involve them in efforts to improve two-way communication between the school and its publics usually reap the rewards of greater confidence in the schools and fewer rumor-caused crises.

Key communicators inform administrators of rumors that are still sparks, allowing them to be easily quelled. Result: no raging fires in the community. Key communicators allow administrators to feel the pulse of the entire community with phone calls to them. Key communicators, because they develop solid rapport with administrators, help the community gain confidence in those administrators.

Once the key communicators are identified, they should be invited to a meeting (breakfast, lunch, or at least coffee and cake) with the principal or with the superintendent.

While the concept should be launched on a districtwide basis, it functions well on a school-by-school basis, particularly in large school districts. Thus, while a superintendent can kick off the program with a luncheon for key communicators from throughout the district to explain the program in detail, individual meetings at the building level will be most productive. Citizens are usually more concerned with what goes on at the local neighborhood school, than with what is happening "downtown" at the district level.

Invitations to local school meetings should be in writing, with a full explanation of the key communicators concept. If you send a letter and follow it with a phone invitation, just about everyone invited will attend the meeting, according to Bagin. In the invitation, emphasize that there will be no more meetings. At the meeting, establish a telephone chain to expedite getting information to them quickly. The meeting should be informal, an hour or less and to the point. Most of all, it should convey the school's appreciation for the service of these key people in the community, and the school's willingness to be open, frank, and honest with its key communicators in return for their help.

CHAPTER EIGHT

New Technology

Once a public information program has been established, and you have surveyed your publics for their information needs, then you must make some decisions on how to communicate with them. While we often talk about "the public" or the "general public," such terms aren't very helpful as we consider public relations planning. There is simply no single, effective way to communicate with the total "public" at once.

Often, people fit into several groups. For example, teachers can also be parents, taxpayers, club members, etc. And parents can be classified as active or non-active. There are many ways to segment and "target" your publics.

Successful communication begins with determining what you want to say, why you want to say it, whom you want to say it to, when you want to say it, and how you want to say it. Getting the act together requires "targeting," either formally or informally.

Targeting involves identifying your purpose in communicating. Do you wish to inform, challenge, affirm, motivate, or question? It also involves identifying your specific public. Are you addressing the school staff, senior citizens, potential volunteers, members of the Hispanic community, legislators, etc.?

The next step is determining what approach will make the most sense to this audience; i.e., persuasion, "plain English," short and sweet, official tone or informal? And, finally, you must figure out the most effective way to deliver your message. Will it be a monthly newsletter, an annual report, a telephone hotline, a series of "town meetings," radio announcements, special presentations on television or a slide-tape or video presentation? Each of these is suited for answering particular communication needs. For example:

Are schools closing because of heavy snow? Radio announcements will work best here. Do parents need to know the dates schools are open, when vacations are scheduled, the monthly date of the PTA meeting? The school calendar is perfect for this. Do you have a special education program where a visual presentation would best convey the enthusiasm of teachers and students alike? A videotape presentation on cable TV could be the key.

A school communicator has a wide range of media to choose from and needs to be familiar with them all. One quick guideline—electronic media are generally best suited for information which must be conveyed quickly; printed is usually more effective when you need details to present your case.

This chapter deals with guidelines for using each.

Age of Technology

No one will deny that the 1980s are the Age of Technology—the Information Age—an age as dramatic as the industrial revolution in its capacity to change the way we live and work.

T. Michael Forney, writing in the March 1982 Public Relations Journal, states that "At some point in the not too distant future, information will be tailored to the individual, reversing a process that Johannes Gutenberg began in the 15th Century. Public audiences will have a wide array of education, entertainment and information choices."

Forney warns, "Enhanced two-way communications systems using cable, satellite, computer and video disc technologies will revolutionize the information transmission and receiving process. As a result, school audiences will become more segmented and specialized, forcing public relations professionals to discard many of the traditional methods used to reach and influence their publics."

The Computer

What has made the technological revolution possible is the computer, more specifically the microcomputer. Using a microcomputer, the school public relations professional can serve the educational community with a far greater impact than at any other time. A microcomputer can be invaluable in saving time, money and energy in a PR office.

Clement J. Cleveland of Pontiac, Mich., a consultant in the areas of computer selection, training and use for educational and business organizations, says a single computer can perform word processing functions as well as do accounting, and carry out a host of public relations functions. It all depends on the software (program) which you have that makes the computer work. Without the software, the microcomputer is practically worthless as it will do little on its own.

"You should consider a microcomputer as much a PR practitioner's tool as a wrench is a plumber's, and purchase one yourself if your district doesn't own one," Cleveland says. Before you buy one, however, you should make a grocery list of things that you may want the machine to do for you. Cleveland suggests these possibilities:

Word Processing

Applying the microprocessor to text writing makes the writing experience a pure joy. No longer do you have to consider typing and re-typing a document through each of its editing stages. The software program should provide easy methods for deleting lines, deleting single words or characters within a word. Inserting characters, words, lines and entire paragraphs in a manuscript need not be a complicated task. Moving or shifting sentences, or even entire sections from top to bottom or within the document, should pose no problem.

There should also be a search and replace function. Aside from the task of creating a document on the screen, the machine will store this document on a floppy disk much like a tape recorder stores the spoken word. At some later date, you enter the proper sequence of commands and you have the ability to retrieve what you have written. Everything will be displayed on the screen.

Once the document has been written, the real value of the microprocessor comes to the fore. First, you can proofread your document for spelling errors with a spelling program. Also, you can examine your document for readability so that you are not writing over the heads of your audience. Third, and this is the biggest payoff; using a specialty, daisy wheel printer, you can print your document in a justified or proportionally spaced mode and use this printout as camera-ready copy for your district's publications. No further typesetting is needed. Just take the printout from your machine printer, paste it on a layout sheet, and you are ready for publication. Considering the cost of typesetting, this final step can quickly repay the investment that you have made in the equipment.

With a little more practice, you can use your word processing program to develop personalized surveys. You select a specific group of people. Write the survey and the machine will cause the printer to automatically address your envelopes, type the letters that you have drafted and print your survey for each person on your mailing list. Everyone will receive the survey as though you had written it solely for each of them, just as though it was a personal letter.

The MODEM

Using a MODEM can greatly expand your computer's capability. A MODEM is a device that links the computer to a telephone. It stands for MOdulator-DEModulator, and it can be either a separate box you plug the phone into or a special board installed in the computer. With a MODEM, you can send and receive electronic mail, join national computer networks such as ED-LINE of the National School Public Relations Assn., or send stories to the printer for typesetting and news releases direct to local news rooms.

"With the telephone-computer connection you can send and receive mail," Clements adds. "This is an excellent wellspring for gaining valuable information on your PR problems. Further, with NSPRA's ED-LINE, education's first electronic network, you can receive accurate, daily news stories of educational happenings throughout the country. If you are a member of the National School Public Relations Assn. and a subscriber to ED-LINE, you are privileged to take what you receive from the network and convert it for your own use within your district. This can amount to the creation of an instant newsletter which could run twice-a-day or at whatever frequency you should determine." You also have access to a wide range of data bases and networks.

Cleveland says computerized typesetting firms are now finding their way into local communities. With a MODEM, you can greatly reduce your typesetting costs, and you can select from thousands of sizes and typefaces with this service. Aside from the actual savings in typesetting costs, you have the ability to control the format of your copy. The real dividend is speed. You can send your copy with the MODEM through the telephone line to the computerized typesetter in a matter of minutes. In almost the same amount of time, the typesetter has the ability to produce camera-ready photo proofsheets.

Other Uses of the Microprocessor

But there are many more uses for the microprocessor which will enhance not only your PR office, but the total school district administration. It will handle:

- ☐ Accounting
- ☐ Maintaining student data
- ☐ Bus scheduling
- ☐ Inventory control
- ☐ Mailing lists
- ☐ Budget preparation
- ☐ Negotiations—document preparation and analysis of economic issues/proposals
- ☐ Bars, graphs, statistical data preparation
- ☐ Student/staff evaluation processes
- ☐ Document preparation for board reports
- ☐ Proofreading of manuscripts
- ☐ Thesaurus use for assistance in manuscript preparation
- ☐ Daily, weekly, monthly and year-end budget summaries
- ☐ Maintaining maintenance schedules on district vehicles

- ☐ Monitoring general/ed, special/ed and categorical funded programs
- ☐ Monitoring student performance data
- ☐ Developing materials needed for finance campaigns
- ☐ Creating charts for monitoring of timelines.

Electronic Media

If you haven't already discovered the nearly limitless potential of video, you should begin today to actively acquaint yourself with the communications vehicle of the '80s. Using video for school public relations purposes will vary according to each school system. Variables include equipment, talent, cooperation with local media and the district's commitment to the use of electronic news gathering equipment.

Cable TV

Cable television is bringing schools into the living rooms of parents and non-parents in ways not possible a few years ago. For schools, television may also provide news to the greatest number in the shortest time for the lowest per-person cost.

Any school district involved with video production should check with area commercial TV stations and cable TV companies to develop an understanding of what they will air or what they require in program content and quality. A serious talk with the program manager of the cable company or television station and a commitment on your part to develop a quality program very often results in a regularly scheduled program time slot.

The Public Relations Society of America (PRSA) predicts that by 1990 there will be 93 million homes in America with a television set and there will be 60 million homes that will be wired for cable. That will be about 64 percent of the country.

Getting Started

If your community has not already awarded its cable TV franchise, there are several benefits your school district might receive as a result of bargaining.

According to The Cable Television Information Center in Washington, D.C., there are certain benefits you might reasonably expect from the cable company at no cost to your district. These include:

- ☐ One exclusive channel for general viewing
- ☐ Equipment necessary to deliver audio and telemetary signals into the cable system
- ☐ A cable drop in each school building and additional drops at cost
- ☐ Access to company facilities, which usually include a full color studio and a mobile van

□ Workshops on production techniques and use of equipment

□ Reasonable amount of maintenance and service.

Even if your community has already awarded its franchise, talk with the company about those basics and there's a strong possibility you'll get them. You might receive the following if more than one company is after your franchise:

□ A full-time person to work with the district on programming

□ Wiring of all classrooms

□ One or more color television receivers for each school

□ A channel on an institutional network linking all school buildings

□ Additional channels as needed

□ Interconnections with other school districts

□ Equipment ranging from a portable camera and recorder to a full color studio

A side benefit from the emergence of cable TV is the effect it is said to be having on the network affiliates. It may be a good idea to revive your contacts with the stations who've been saying "no" all this time. The pressure from cable is causing them to do a turnaround.

Program Ideas

One way to use cable TV while helping the superintendent to improve the school district's internal and external communications is through a twice weekly talk show. For example, the Garland (Texas) school system produces a 30-minute program, "Meet the Superintendent." The program is either taped at the cable company's studio with the superintendent and guests, or is taped on location at one of the district's facilities to feature a special program. The shows have dealt with the district's goals, the communications efforts of the district, personnel practices, athletics, instructional resources and curriculum. Other districts have student magazine format programs and news shows. Many videotape classroom sessions for cable broadcast.

Cable TV programming produced about the school system is usually of interest to the entire community. Story ideas might include:

□ Schools in action; debates, plays, science fairs, concerts, art exhibits, sports events and instructional programs such as students "learning to read," math, foreign language, etc.

□ Student news shows

□ School "hotline"—monthly or weekly shows with the superintendent, principals, teachers and other staff members answering "tough" questions from viewers

□ Series of documentaries of critical school issues like budget, funding, test scores, declining enrollment, school closings

□ Calendar of events

□ List of school award winners—students selected for scholarships, community awards, special honors.

The Janesville (Wis.) school system purchased $3,000 worth of portable video equipment a few years ago and has been "on location" ever since. Howard Gage, coordinator of public information, began producing action programs which are shown during halftime on the local cable company's televised high school football and basketball games. He is building up a library of 30 video productions a year.

In addition to cablecasting the programs, Gage shows them to the school board, service clubs, PTAs, teachers and special interest groups. He sometimes presses students or staff members into service to assist in running the camera. The cable company furnishes editing facilities which allow him to give a professional look to the finished product. The portable equipment is also used by the public information office to produce staff in-service programs, maintenance reports to the board of education and the superintendent's messages to the staff.

Commercial Television

The communications exposure usually most sought after by school districts and least achieved, unless there's some kind of crisis, is coverage on TV news. Unfortunately, far too few school districts realize the "givens" of TV news coverage, the parameters within which TV assignment editors must operate.

The fact is that after you get the "big story"—mishaps, violence, politics, taxes, the economy, protests, courts and the like—out of the way, then add sports, weather and commercials, there isn't much left in a newscast.

What's not left is time to cover routine school district functions like art displays, school plays and science fairs. Everyone has science fairs. If a station covers one, it's inundated in following days by complaints from dozens of schools whose science fairs remained in obscurity. The only way, usually, to get a science fair covered on TV is to have a student develop a new formula for the neutron bomb or accidentally blow a hole in the chemistry lab wall!

Yet, there are plenty of human interest stories that TV stations will cover if the information on them is packaged and presented to them properly.

The key to "getting on television news" is to be timely, topical, visual and different from the everyday routine. Educators must face the fact that except in unusual circumstances they simply are not going to attract many TV cameras. Therefore, to get TV coverage in the absence of controversy, you must plan the kinds of offbeat, people-oriented, highly

Getting on TV

□ Don't send a three-page, single-spaced news release to a TV station and expect someone to wade through it to try to determine what it's all about. More often than not, it will be consigned to the waste basket.

□ Do send a brief, to-the-point, "who, what, when, where and why" memo to the proper person (usually the assignment editor) and follow it up with a telephone call.

□ Concentrate on stories with a human interest angle such as hundreds of students releasing green helium-filled balloons to the winds, each containing a message to the community conveying concern for the starving children of the world or "good news" about their schools.

□ Emphasize timely stories such as mock presidential elections in advance of the real thing.

□ Set up interesting debates such as mock United Nations debates concerning critical world issues, or on a topic of critical community concern.

□ Stress colorful, highly visible stories including Flag Day and other holiday and patriotic pageants; ethnic dress, dances and songs on days honoring various heritages.

visual feature stories that tie closely to community interests or to area, state or national events or topics of debate. Tie local stories to national issues such as the annual Gallup Poll of Public Attidtudes about public schools. What do local people believe about their schools?

Annual Report on TV

Because television has become the means identified by most adults as their primary source of information, it should be considered as the means for presenting school district information such as the annual report to a wide public. John Cone, executive director of the South Carolina School Boards Assn., says it has clear advantages.

1. The cost of using television is comparable to buying newspaper space.

2. Those who cannot or will not read your annual report can and probably will sit and listen to an attractive televised report. Some will tune out the station but this can be minimized with the right kind of advance publicity and an entertaining format.

3. Thousands of citizens have an opportunity to see and hear the superintendent as he presents the "state of the schools" address.
4. The viewer can look at a chart and have it explained. Nothing is more frustrating than seeing a graph in the written annual report and not being able to understand what it means.
5. Through the use of film shot on site the viewers can actually see what is happening in the schools. They are reminded of how small a five-year-old child is. They can see vocational students operating a printing press. They may see for the first time how crowded a classroom can be. They can see enthusiastic teachers and motivated students.
6. Others can appear live on the air and question what the school spokesperson has said. A news team can lend credibility to the report by interviewing the superintendent on the air. This technique may be an immediate answer to questions which naturally arise in the minds of the viewers as the report progresses.
7. The programs can be taped, stored and reviewed year after year. A sense of continuity develops when the spokesperson can say "Here is what we promised you three years ago and here is what we have done." When excerpts of previous reports are used they lend an atmosphere of long-range planning and commitment to openness and candor.

Guides for Planning

Cam Keyser, audio-visual consultant and former information specialist for the Charlotte-Mecklenberg (N.C.) schools, says there are several production questions which should be answered when planning to broadcast an annual report: Where will you secure the crew, equipment and expertise to have your show produced? Whom do you know well enough to ask? How much do you know about television production and how much more are you willing to learn?

Local cable systems with their emphasis on public access are excellent potential production sources, Keyser says. Consider, also, college/university broadcasting departments, corporate in-house video departments, independent TV producers, or even the local PBS or commercial television station.

When planning to broadcast an annual report, there are some general caution signs to be observed:

☐ Don't pay to have the report published in the paper and then expect the television stations to donate air time.
☐ Check the rating books to see which station or stations should broadcast your report, how much you should pay them and when your audience is watching.

- [ ] Don't ask several stations for a simulcast. They will probably refuse and even if they agree, robbing the TV audience of a choice of programs may make your viewers angry.
- [ ] Make sure everyone involved in taping the program understands that its content is confidential. A leak to a news staff can destroy your chances for a good audience.
- [ ] Plan the release of the information so that the news coverage works for and not against your program.
- [ ] Make certain that you have some important, hard news to release through the annual report.

Remember that in a broadcast production, you are not creating an annual financial report; although, surely, some of that information can—and should—be a part. What you want to create is a mood—an impression—a feeling about your school system and the good things it has going for it. You're creating a people report and setting the tone for an image.

Remember Radio

With the coming of cable TV, communication satellites, video discs, laser beam and other technological advances in electronic communications, radio took somewhat of a back seat for a while. Yet, the great majority of communities in the nation aren't serviced by their own TV or cable TV stations. And most productive TV advertising costs a great deal even when it is available on a local basis. Or, if it's a bargain, it's usually on a station with a small viewing audience.

On the other hand, ask your friends and neighbors how many of them listen each day, at one time or another, to a local radio station. Ask how many senior citizens, retired persons, housewives and a wide variety of people at work listen to the radio, particularly to radio talk shows. The answer, in many communities, is astounding. Thousands of urban workers driving in the highway gridlocks each morning and evening are captive audiences for radio programs.

There are several avenues of free radio communication available to the school district trying to enhance its public image, and for that matter, there is also paid radio advertising that reaches a great many people for a reasonably small investment.

One avenue of radio communications available to school districts is the telephone talk show. Here a little person-to-person contact between the school district and the call-in host or the show's producer can lead to interesting and informative live interviews of school district personnel on the air, either in the studio or on the telephone, followed by a question-and-answer session involving callers listening to the show.

So the talk show wants controversy? Fine! Volunteer to have capable, knowledgeable school district personnel field questions about sex education, censorship, school closings and whatever is a "hot item" at the time.

Any capable school district spokesperson, given the opportunity on a radio show reaching out across the community, should have little trouble explaining calmly and objectively, to an attentive, captive audience, the rationale behind school system policy and procedures, even when they deal with a controversial, emotional issue.

Public Service Announcements

Another key means of radio communication, available particularly to the public sector, is the public service announcement. Here, a radio station sets aside normally paid advertising time for free announcements as a public service.

There are primarily two ways of taking advantage of this opportunity. One is to prepare a script, and send it to the station's general manager or community relations director and ask that it be recorded by station personnel and used on the air.

1. **Script.** Scripts should be prepared in times of 10, 20, and 30-second announcements on a topic of public interest—board meeting dates, school activities, report card dates, parent involvement programs, calls for volunteers and many more.

2. **Record spots.** A considerably more effective way is to record the spots yourself with air-quality equipment, catchy script, a good voice and some background music. Take them to the radio station ready for the air. This effort could mean the difference between a seldom-used spot and a lively, attention-getting, prime-time announcement on behalf of your school district.

Some personal contact with the person at the station responsible for public service announcements will quickly establish the desired format, necessary technological information and other station requirements.

In any case, school districts preparing public service spots should evaluate the script with four basic questions. They are:

1. Does the opening line attract attention?
2. Is the body of the announcement informative, short and to the point, and does it keep the interest alive?

20 Do's and Don'ts for Newslines

1. Investigate the possibility of getting a special telephone number—perhaps one with a special significance—perhaps one with your district's initials as an acronym.
2. Install an outside telephone line exclusively for your newsline. If callers have to go through the switchboard, they won't be able to get news at night or when you're using the phone during the day.
3. Write for the ear rather than the eye when preparing newsline messages. People have to be able to tell immediately what you're talking about. Use short sentences and an informal, conversational style. Listen to radio or television news announcers for tips on phrasing introductions and on presentation.
4. Practice to get the hang of timing, inflection, expression. And do read over the message before you record it. Very few people are poised enough to get by with recording an unrehearsed message.
5. Listen to each message before you release it to the public. Something that looked fine on paper may not sound good.
6. Avoid making your pitch too slick. The hard-sell, "we're-the-greatest" ap-

proach is even more grating on the telephone than on paper.
7. Do worry about the quality of reproduction. A poor, fuzzy or scratchy recording that's hard to decipher will turn off most callers. If the quality of your recording is poor, tell the company that supplied it. Telephone your newsline yourself periodically to double check on the quality.
8. Devise a standard opening and closing so people can readily identify what they're listening to. (You'll get wrong numbers, just like any other phone line does.)
9. Avoid misunderstanding, especially on events reported in advance, by using the designation "on Tuesday" rather than "tomorrow" or "day after tomorrow."
10. Notify the news media of your service. Perhaps a local radio station may be interested in taping the message for daily broadcast. The newsline is a handy way of keeping the media informed of district happenings.
11. Conduct a massive publicity campaign when you initiate your newsline service, but don't stop there. People need to be reminded constantly if you want them to call regularly.

Promote the newsline in every district publication or other regular information service.

12. Meet your schedule. If you promise daily news, you're obligated to come through. You'll quickly lose listeners if you aren't dependable.

13. Believe there is enough news to provide it daily. You don't need a new topic every day. Update a previous story. Explain the whys behind your school policies and procedures. Announce upcoming school events. List the entire calendar of events for a week or month. Do a mini-feature on something especially interesting, unusual or successful going on in a classroom. Provide some statistics about your district, such as total number of students or staff members, numbers of new teachers, enrollment trends, even the number of school buses and students who ride them.

14. Make every effort to cover hard news before you use a feature or filler. News should be your number one priority.

15. Cover your problems or crises as soon as they occur. If you don't know the whole story, say so and comment on what you do know. Otherwise, you've lost probably the most important asset of your news-line—immediacy.

16. Cover the results of school board meetings and negotiating sessions as soon as possible. You can record board meeting results before you go home after the meeting, providing early-rising staff members with a 6 a.m. report. That's service.

17. Repeat a timeless or especially important message, if necessary; but reword it. Use a new introduction or add new information.

18. Retract or correct when you make a mistake. It lends substantially to credibility—to say nothing of protecting you from lawsuits.

19. Keep your messages short. Most people can't take listening to something prerecorded for more than three minutes.

20. Keep a calendar to suggest topics for future messages. Forthcoming meetings, school holidays, and other seasonal topics are naturals—such as when the budget process begins, when negotiating sessions begin, when test socres come out. And do anticipate devoting one day's message to answering the questions people ask each year: "Do we have a holiday for Columbus Day?" "Do we get out early at Thanksgiving?"

3. Is the closing forceful and does it demand, or suggest, some kind of action on the part of the listener?
4. Is a phone number or address for responding included?

Hotline Information

But there are still other tools to get the school story across to the community. One of these is the telephone newsline. Some school districts call it a "hotline" or an "informaphone" or a "telecom" service. But whatever it's called, it is usually effective in getting up-to-date messages out to the community.

Making A Newsline Work

☐ Keep the recorded messages to 90 seconds or less. About 80 percent of the messages are 60 seconds or less.

☐ Attempt to include only news of areawide or districtwide interest, although a smaller district could consider including local school items.

☐ Include agendas of area advisory committees, agendas of board of education meetings, and brief summaries of news releases issued from the central office, as appropriate.

☐ Change the message two to three times each week.

☐ Prerecord tapes announcing school closings in bad weather which can be put on early (5-6 a.m.) to notify area news media.

☐ Consider carrying the daily elementary school lunch menus. This often is a high interest item.

Audiovisuals

Another PR tool growing in usage is the audiovisual presentation, whether it be slides, a slide-tape, film, or videotape.

One of the most common presentations over the years has been the slide-tape presentation, preferably done automatically, with music and voice, complementing an attractive display of slides, flashing or fading on and off on anywhere up to a half dozen screens.

There usually is nothing deadlier than the one-person, one-slide-at-a-time, monotone description approach. Audiences more than likely will be restless at best as they wait for the ordeal to end, or, at worst, downright insulted.

A well-done 16 mm film or videotape, on the other hand, makes a fine audiovisual. The problem with motion pictures, however, is that they are expensive and extremely difficult to produce. Done in cooperation with local businesses, chambers of commerce or other civic groups contributing funds for production, they can be very effective.

A good 16-mm color film can cost an absolute minimum of $2,000 a minute to produce, and that's if you can get a free lance producer who needs the work.

More and more school districts today are switching to the production of videotaped programs which can be produced for cable television, and then copied for showing before community groups.

Yet, a good, even dazzling, 15-minute slide-tape, using slides that most school districts already have, can be put together in house for a few hundred dollars.

It's important, however, to get someone who is experienced with the whole process and creative enough to blend words, music and slides into a colorful, fast-moving and informative presentation.

Most school districts have many such persons right in the ranks of their teachers and administrators; persons who would be flattered to be asked to put their audiovisual skills to work to help the school district tell its story to the community.

Give them a script (prepared by the school information officer or someone else with writing talent), a couple of hundred slides of kids, and a few charts and graphs, and you will be amazed at what kind of high-impact community message they can put together.

The staff of the Eastman Kodak Education Center at Riverwood, Rochester, N.Y., presents the following tips for putting together a good audiovisual presentation:

Keep your objective:
□ Be audience-oriented, not subject-oriented, when planning your material. Make a careful analysis of what you are trying to accomplish with the presentation.
□ Decide what you want the audience to do after seeing the presentation. Do you want to change its attitudes? Do you want action on the part of the audience? Is the presentation solely informational? What degree of increase in audience understanding is required?

Audience Analysis:
□ Size. If a large group, you need a wider variety of examples, a broader, less intimate approach.
□ Occupations and education. Age and sex. Is it a voluntary or captive audience?
□ Plan your material. Don't be too elementary, but don't talk over your audience's heads. How much material is appropriate to this kind of group? What are the best ways to get it across, considering the components of this specific audience?
□ Audience attitude. Is it likely to be hostile or supportive? Does it have anxieties about your subject? What are these anxieties? What beliefs do they already have about your subject? Are these accurate or misinformed? Do they have prejudices which must be dispelled?

Materials Preparation:
□ File cards. Put all ideas on file cards, one idea per card, using sketchy words and trying to think visually. Don't worry about the number of cards. Edit, delete and organize into one kind of order, either chronologically, by subject, or whatever suits your material best.
□ Prepare your verbal presentation, following the file card ideas you have decided to

use. Time your presentation and adjust it to desired length. Allow time for questions and answers. Look for ways to get occasional audience response (like raising hands to a question).

☐ Prepare visuals to go with your file card ideas. 2 x 2 slides are good. Also movie sequences. Frequently let the visual tell the story without spoken words. Sometimes put words on slides, especially to indicate lead ideas or summary points. Use symbols, charts, diagrams, interspersed with slides. Variety is very effective.

☐ Avoid verbal and visual detail, long captions and extraneous detail.

☐ Don't explain the obvious. Let the charts and graphs speak for themselves.

☐ Make each visual tell an important story; don't use more than you need. Mix long shots, medium shots and closeups. Use close-ups sparingly for impact.

☐ Avoid bars and lines in graphs. Instead, use pictorial comparisons. Good visuals don't require great ability. Originality and creativity are important.

☐ Lettering and gimmicks: titles can be objects (pencils, for instance) formed into letters, then a slide of it.

Presentation:

☐ Use your visuals for cues rather then depending on a written sheet. You can, if you practice.

☐ Study your environment carefully. Think about screen size and location; lighting control; sound system; ventilation. All of these can affect the mood of the audience.

☐ Rehearse the complete presentation, with visuals. Aim for a conversational tone of voice. Don't memorize the material word for word.

☐ Time the presentation. Remember there are more famous short speeches than long ones.

☐ Check the projection equipment and have an extra bulb on hand.

☐ Arrive early to be sure everything works and to give you time to relax.

CHAPTER NINE

Printing Your Own Story

There is little doubt that a school district that relies on the media or on word of mouth to spread positive news about the schools is in deep trouble. The very nature of both these modes of communication is to do exactly the opposite.

Thus, a school district has to tell its own positive story, and one of the best ways to do it—by far—is in print.

The District Newsletter

That's not to say a school district newsletter, an annual report or other printed communication should be nothing more than a propaganda sheet. That's almost as bad as nothing at all. But an honest, factual, attractive and inexpensive newsletter is essential in the telling of the school district story.

Ideally, such a newsletter should be sent to every resident in the district. But when the size of the district prohibits such distribution, it must at least go to employees, parents and community leaders—people who must know the positive aspects of public education today if public confidence is to be restored.

A word of caution: many newsletter editors seem to forget they are competing for readership. When the school publication goes up against the reader's choices it frequently loses because it is not attractive, concise and worth the reader's investment of time. School editors need to remember that they compete for the readership of the community audience with their newsletter.

And by newsletter it is meant a **letter with news** about what is going on in the schools.

For far too many years, the prototype school district newsletter consisted of a small, four-page publication on slick paper, the most prominent part of which was a page-one "Message from the Superintendent," which featured some high sounding, dollar-and-a-quarter words of education philosophy, coupled with a reminder that this was the best school district in the universe.

Rarely was there any substantive news involved, and more often than not the prose—or at least the part of it that could be understood—was pure "puff."

Thankfully, the format of many school district newspapers has changed dramatically. Many are now breezy, informative tabloids, with plenty of features about what's going on in the schools. They have involved content—more pictures, more white space, more eye-catching layouts. And they have changed, in the style of the writing.

> Perhaps no more formidable barrier to better communications by educators has ever existed than the language of "pedagese," the special hieroglyphics of the pedagogue; the traditional, formal language of educational treatises, since the dawn of the doctoral thesis.

Annual Report

Another major publication that helps tell the community about the school district is the annual report. Although annual reports appear to be dying out in some districts, they are now being mandated by law in several states—not only at the district level, but for each school building.

An annual report should be positive. It should list school district accomplishments. It should proudly promote the district's outstanding features. But it should never attempt to cover up weaknesses or to pretend that they do not exist.

A good annual report is one that seeks the credibility of its community, promotes the good, admits the bad and tells what the school district is going to do to turn the latter into the former.

The format of the annual report varies widely. In some communities, the report is a special publication that stands by itself. In others it is an insert in a local newspaper or in the school district's annual calendar or in its community newsletter. Many are using videotape for release on cable TV or developing slide-tape productions.

The first point to be considered, though, when considering an annual report, is its cost.

A school district that is having financial problems—and most are—can be criticized severely, and rightfully so, for putting out an elaborate and expensive annual report at the same time it is closing schools, laying off teachers and cutting back on the athletic program.

For that matter, the days of the slick, four-color, big corporation look-alike annual report for any school district are long past, unless every penny of the production comes from a source other than school district funds.

But regardless of the format used, or the cost involved, the best "print" annual reports share most of the following characteristics:

- ☐ **An overall theme.** This could be the "people of your district" with a review of each department and school and how it operates. The theme could review an advisory committee's report on recommended curriculum changes and how the board hopes to implement them.
- ☐ **A special section dealing with the budget**—how much is needed for the year, with costs broken down into major categories.
- ☐ **Lots of photos**—to personalize the report for readers.
- ☐ **Highlights of the past year**—provide background, and special goals (of the board, superintendent or individual schools and depart-

Tips for Annual Reports

1. **Time is of the essence.** Hair styles change. Clothing styles change. Even the methods educators use to teach are changing. Deliberately plan your pictures to capture the excitement and motion of learning so that they will have a "timelessness" to them, if possible. Avoid the time element that can enter into your story.

2. **Get help.** Corporations often hire an advertising firm to help them do their annual report. A volunteer photographer, or a student photographer, can help tremendously. Other educators can give you suggestions for pictures and for story, or copy block, ideas. Have someone whose opinions you value be your sounding board. Maybe you have a big taxpayer corporation in your district. Their PR department might be willing to help you.

3. **Color costs.** Each extra color you use in your layout means an extra press run. Labor and production costs zoom. A printer you trust can give you invaluable advice about the proper use of extra color.

4. **Read and proof copy, again and again.** Different copy readers and different proofreaders at different stages of production will help you find the small errors that always seem to crop up. Find good ones and use them. Also, you can examine your document for readability so that you are not writing over the heads of your audience. Eliminate all jargon.

ments) for the next 12 months are stated. These help focus people's attention on priority issues which may change from year to year.
- □ **Results of achievement tests or assessment**—detailed and explained with special reference to major outcomes or findings. Plans to correct weaknesses should be discussed.
- □ **Problem areas of the system**—dealt with openly and fairly. If the system has to suffer through an employee strike or violence in a school, the issue is met head-on and what steps have been or will be taken to avoid difficulty in the future are covered.
- □ **Wide distribution** throughout the community via the mail, local schools, realtors, visitors' centers, chambers of commerce, churches, libraries and other means.

School Calendar

Still another printed publication used broadly by school districts as a communication tool is the annual school district calendar. A wall calendar for the entire school year can be many things to many people.
- □ It can remind parents, month by month, of important dates—board meetings, PTA meetings, school visitations, sports schedules, report card dates, etc.
- □ It can give a school district good year-round exposure; hanging in thousands of homes throughout the district, containing important dates and general information about the schools, it reminds parents, day-by-day that the school district cares to communicate with them.
- □ It can be a reference guide to parents for school district rules, regulations and policies.

Calendars are relatively expensive to print, and time-consumning to plan and put together, but a good one can well be worth the effort by reaping communication rewards from the community.

Many school districts are finding funding for calendar printing from local banks, realtors or businesses. A small credit line affixed on the bottom of the final page is usually all the civic-minded group wants or expects and the benefits to them and the schools are far reaching.

Specialized Publications

Besides newsletters, annual reports and calendars, school districts can use any number of specialized publications to enhance their communication efforts. Among the most used are:

Board Meeting Brochure

First-time visitors to a board meeting will find such a brochure of value. They can learn how the board operates and how a citizen can pose questions and suggestions to the board. Photos of board members and district officials, along with brief biographies, personalize the system's leaders.

This brochure is usually supplemented by an agenda of proposed business, with brief statements of background for each item. Visitors then know what is being discussed or voted upon as the meeting progresses.

Speakers Bureau

This brochure is used to stimulate community clubs and associations to schedule a school official to speak before their membership. The brochure contains a list of possible speakers and titles of presentations they have prepared. Details as to how a speaker can be obtained are included. Copies are sent every year to presidents and program chairpersons of community groups. The brochure should be updated annually.

Pre-School Orientation

Parents of children about to enter pre-kindergarten, kindergarten, or first grade, usually have many questions about the school's instructional program in the early grades. This kind of publication (tied in with an in-school orientation visit) should help prepare parents and their youngsters for the new experience. Details are provided about daily activities, the instructional program, transportation, health factors, reporting of pupil progress, joint teacher-parent programs, etc.

Basic Facts

Many large districts find a single reference booklet covering all aspects of the system of value to staff members and interested citizens. Content may cover personnel, pupils, finances, facilities, course offerings, special projects and community information. Copies should be provided to community leaders and prospective staff members. Such a booklet can also save research time for staff members who answer questions from the public. This is frequently printed in wallet size for handy reference.

Directories

Staff members as well as interested citizens appreciate a well-indexed, district directory of employees, schools, facilities and community and governmental agencies. Content may include maps and personnel directories by departments and schools. Officers of educational associations and committees can be listed.

Internal

Of all the publications developed by a school district or agency perhaps none are as important as those designed for internal audiences—the professional and support staff members. For these publics are the real ambassadors of any school district. They are the ones who are seen as the true information source by the majority of residents. "They have the answers—they work there," is the frequently heard comment. Such publications include **staff weekly bulletins** and newsletters, "Board Notes" the morning following each meeting of the board of education, and local school building newsletters.

Guidelines For Good Writing

Accompanying the memorandum was a collection of seven guidelines for clear writing, developed by Donald Hymes, district director of media, technology and production, (with a nod to *Writer's Digest*), which the superintendent suggested his staff keep "close at hand".

Good writing is good writing no matter what the subject is, the attachment began, and good writers do not change their styles whether they're writing home or composing a treatise on education. Whether you're composing a memo to your staff or a report to the board of education, the purpose of the document is to communicate, not to demonstrate your intellect or eloquence. So every time you write anything, look it over before you send it on.

Keep in mind the following guidelines:

☐ Prefer the plain word to the fancy. Telling a mother that her child is a "marginal underachiever" may make you sound erudite, but she'd know better what you meant if you said the child was "a little slow."

☐ Prefer the familiar word to the unfamiliar. If you need a Thesaurus to find a word, don't use it. It should be one that comes naturally. And, most important, it should be familiar to the receiver of the message, not just to the writer. Know your audience and don't overestimate either their reading level or their desire to plow through your prose.

Check your Writing Style

Perhaps a story from the Montgomery County (Md.) Public Schools reported in *IT STARTS in the Classroom* several years ago gives some solid rules of clear writing for school district administrators, teachers, writers and editors throughout the country:

It all started with an innocent request. At the end of an administrative workshop for the Montgomery County Schools, information officer Kenneth Muir invited the participants to pass along suggestions for improving communication.

☐ Never use a long word when a short one will do as well. "Assistance" means "help"; "indicate" means "say"; "innovative" means "new". Words of three syllables or more raise your writing's *Fog Index* and hide your meaning.

☐ Never use two (or more) words when one will do as well. "Within the near future" means "soon"; "due to the fact that" means "because". Take the common phrase "in order to." Knock off the first two words and ask yourself if it changes the meaning at all. Look at all your phrases the same way.

☐ Master the simple declarative sentence and use it—often. A sentence, by definition, has a subject, a verb and an object. Too often, however, sentences have too many of each—guaranteeing that the reader will get lost in the maze.

☐ Cut out needless words, sentences and paragraphs. If it doesn't add to your meaning, you don't need it. Some people think that the longer the message, the more important it seems. Actually, it often works the other way around. Long paragraphs intimidate readers, and unnecessary words and phrases can muddle the meaning.

☐ Revise and rewrite. Improvement is always possible. There isn't a writer alive who won't benefit from a little editing, starting with his or her own pencil.

There was, in fact, only one response, but it sparked a movement in the school system that may have lasting repercussions. It took the form of an anonymous letter (signed "The Curmudgeon") that criticized the superintendent's "tendency to use pedantic prose."

"Often the superintendent's ideas are drowned by his words," the letter said. "If he wanted to tell us that when the cat's away, the mice will play, it would come out something like this: 'Rodents, in the absence of their feline adversaries, are prone to divert themselves.' What comes across is, 'I don't want to really communicate with you.' " The letter suggested that before a memo goes out, someone in the information office should "translate" it into concise English. "If after the obfuscation has been wiped away there's a blank piece of paper," the letter concluded, "that says something, too."

A note like this could have blown the roof off the administration building, but Muir saw it as a chance to promote it as one of his pet crusades. And the superintendent went along enthusiastically. A few days later, a memorandum went out to the administration staff, quoting "The Curmudgeon's" letter, and admitting that "my written and spoken language is frequently both formal and pedantic." Although a 20-year custom of using language that is too formal might be hard to break, the superintendent went on, "my habit patterns may stand in the way of good communication." So, he promised, "I'm going to try to do better."

The superintendent noted that he wasn't the only offender. "My impression from reading hundreds of staff memoranda is that this problem is of epidemic proportions." To those who think that this style is what the superintendent wants, he said, "let me take this opportunity to assure you that it is not. Rather, I urge you to join me in an effort to frame our thoughts in the most clear and concise language possible."

A Readership Survey

How do you know if your newsletter is good?
□ Ask your readers. The best way to find out how your newsletter is being received is to give your readers the chance to tell you. Solicit mailed comments, perhaps with a little questionnaire form in one issue a year. Ask for comments at a PTA meeting. Make random phone calls to parents. Don't do your work in a vacuum.
□ Feedback, both good and bad, may come without solicitation, too. So make sure the name and address and telephone number of the editor is prominently displayed on the newsletter.

Story Ideas

Research has shown that the most read stories in a school newsletter are stories about students. There isn't anything more exciting than capturing a child who is in the process of learning. What this boils down to is that you have at your disposal a natural actor in a child, an expected result in the learning process and a guaranteed interest in your education program because your readers are investing hard-earned dollars in it.

There are literally hundreds of stories found in school buildings everyday. All you need to remember is that as long as school is in session there is learning and where there is learning there is a story.

Yet, the problem remains of how to uncover these stories that take place daily throughout the school district.

Media Tip Sheet

Oxford Public Schools

Public Information Department

There will be a news story happening in my classroom. . .

Who is involved:

What it is about:

When will it happen:

Where will it happen:

How will it be carried out:

Is there anything unusual or unique about this story:

From:

School:

Grade:

Room:

Leave completed form with your building principal.

> Thank you for your cooperation,
> Jane Smith
> Public Information

One solution is a "tip" sheet that can be sent monthly to each teacher in each school, asking them to submit story ideas for the district's newsletter. And you might name a newsletter representative in each school

Printing Guidelines

1. **Know your printer.** Even if you have to choose him or her through open bidding, assure yourself that the shop is capable of producing the kind of material you envision. If you're not familiar with the shop's work, insist on samples being submitted with the bid.

2. **Know the capabilities of the shop's equipment.** If the presses have a sheet capacity of 8½ x 11, or 17 x 22½, a 6 x 9 booklet can cost you almost twice as much as one that is 5½ x 8½. Understand that on a 17½ x 22½ inch sheet, you can print 16 pages of 5½ x 8½. If you ask to do a 20-page book, you will be paying quite a premium for those extra four pages, because they require extra cutting, folding and collating. For the same reason, you may find that a 60-page brochure will cost more than a 64-pager. Know what kind of bindery equipment is available. If it has to be contracted out you will have to pay the printer a profit on top of what is paid to the bindery. And if the shop has only one-color presses, a two-color job requires two press runs, and will cost quite a bit more than at a printer who has two-color presses.

3. **Write specifications carefully and clearly.** They should cover these items.

   □ Weight, color and quality of paper for text cover. Name the exact stock you want, or note "or equivalent." Insist on samples to be submitted with bid.

   □ Page size, number of pages and quality of run. If type hasn't been set, and you're not sure how many pages there will be, estimate and ask for prices by 4-page or 8-page sections above and below your estimate. If there is a possibility you may need more copies than you specify, ask for cost of additional hundreds or thousands.

   □ Number of ink colors, specifying if other than black and where color is to be—on all pages, certain pages, etc. If you can restrict your second color to one section, you can

whose job it is to remind teachers to turn in the tip sheets and to follow through on story ideas.

save money and still have a colorful looking book.

□ Amount of copy and heads and what typeface and head styles you want. Use the typefaces the printer has, because if he jobs out the typesetting, you pay more.

□ Time requirements. Specify when you will deliver the copy and how long the printer has to complete the job. How long will you be allowed to keep the proofs? Is the printer able to use the electronic transfer method for typesetting, enabling you to send your copy via a MODEM and thus, eliminating the cost of typesetting?

□ Number of halftones (photographs), duotones or color separations, and where they will be used.

□ Other services to be provided by the printer, such as artwork, composition, addressing, mailing, packaging or slip-sheeting and delivery.

□ Your cost if you make changes after the blueline proof.

□ Anything unusual, such as die-cuts, embossing or foldouts.

Failing to include any of these items in your bid or your contract can cost you a disproportionate premium if you add them in midstream.

4. **Make sure your copy is neat and your instructions are clear.** Changes required because the printer didn't understand what you wanted can be billed to you as author's corrections. If you want a picture cropped a certain way, do it yourself with a grease pencil in the margin. Don't assume the printer will do anything automatically. Put it in writing.

5. **Prepare a dummy.** Don't make the printer guess what you want to go where.

6. **Check proofs carefully and quickly.** Have more than one person read them. Resist the temptation to edit it again at this stage, because it will cost you.

7. **Insist that the printer stick to his/her promises only if you have stuck to yours.**

Getting It Printed

Working with your printer is a key to producing quality school district publications. Jonathan W. Seybold and his father opened the first non-newspaper computerized phototypesetting shop in the world in 1963. In an interview with *Communications Briefings,* Seybold sees the future for in-house typesetting: brand new computer printers combining laser and photocopier technologies linked with powerful microcomputers running sophisticated typesetting software. New systems, Seybold says, allow users to establish page formats and almost "pour" their text into place, filling columns, inserting rules (lines) and leaving blanks where photos will go later.

Making It Look Good

The design of your publication should strive for clarity and simplicity. One design idea to use is the 30-3-30 theory. Lay out your publication and newsletter for the page flipper (the 30-second reader), the scanner (the three-minute reader), and the in-depth reader who reads your entire 30-minute publication. And keep in mind that most readers fall in the first two categories.

Educators often put too much copy and too many photos on one page. A general rule for special topic publications is to keep at least 20-30 percent of each two-page spread open for "breathing room."

Some tips on graphics include:

☐ Body copy should be 9, 10, or 11 pt. in a serif typeface. Spacing (called leading) between lines and columns of copy needs to be adequate to avoid the crowded look.

☐ Copy lines should be no longer than two alphabets or 52 characters. Many readers prefer a copy column about three inches in width or shorter.

☐ Photographs can add punch to your publication. But make sure they are worth printing and help tell the action story of your program. Words of caution: bad photographs are worse than no photographs at all.

☐ Use copy-breaking devices to disarm a wave of gray in your publication. Box copy with rules, use subheads, shades of a color, and use bold breakouts when applicable.

☐ Don't print over designs in the belief that a special effect will be created. Usually, you make your publication more difficult to read.

☐ Don't use many type families in the same publication unless you want to start a printing business for a circus.

☐ Use sans serif type for headlines.

☐ As a general rule, never use less than 8 point or more than 36 point type in any 8-1/2 by 11 inch publication.

Selecting Paper

Most school publications are printed on 60 lb. offset "house paper" which is usually an excellent match for newsletter and other publications. Some other characteristics of paper you need to know are:

- □ Weight is calculated to a ream (500 sheets).
- □ Brightness is important because a bright white sheet reflects more light, improves the contrast range and therefore improves the quality of any photographs which may be used.
- □ Opacity is an important characteristic when you are printing on both sides of the page. Lightweight papers usually show through and create readability problems.
- □ Surface is an important characteristic especially when printing photographs. Rough-surfaced paper will absorb more ink and leave dark areas gray and dull.

Distribution . . . to the Readers

Once you've completed your publication or newsletter, you need to make sure your readers receive it. Some distribution methods are:

- □ Distribute to all school employees first. They need to know about your program so they can tell others.
- □ Use direct mail through the post office. You can qualify for a non-profit, bulk rate permit which is the least expensive postage of the U.S. Postal Service. Get to know your local post office customer service person and see what needs to be done to determine if this delivery system is the best one for you.
- □ Use a school group like the marching band or a community scouting group to distribute your publication.

These groups are always looking for fund-raising ideas and this method is less expensive than the postal service.

- □ Drop off quantities at public spots throughout the community. See if you can get grocery store managers to drop one in the grocery bag of each customer.
- □ Insert your publication in the local newspaper or buy space for your publication.
- □ Distribution through students is usually the worst method. After about the fifth grade, they usually don't make it home and you usually alienate custodians and bus drivers because of the extra "trash" created by your publication.

CHAPTER TEN

Working with the Media

An education reporter from an urban daily newspaper went to work for the city's school district as an information specialist.

After only a couple of months on the job, he called his former boss—an editor with whom he had been close—to complain, gently, of the negative coverage the paper had been giving the school district.

"Listen," the editor said, "the people you work for are educators. They're supposed to be educating kids. They're paid by the taxpayers to educate kids. When they do, that's not news. That's what they're paid to do. It's when they don't that it's news."

That, unfortunately—or fortunately, if you're looking at it from the perspective of the media—is a true story.

It is the primary reason why, in far too many instances, the educator and the reporter get along like the cobra and the mongoose. And it is the bane of the existence of the school PR specialist.

Journalism Under Fire?

It might be argued by some that the press and all institutions are under attack by a public that finds them too big, too arrogant and too unaccountable.

The press, by its nature, is rarely beloved—nor should that be its aim. Too often it must be the bearer of bad tidings. While the complaints against the press are diverse, they most often center around such questions as whether reporters are fair and objective and whether you can believe what you read and see.

Most school board members and many superintendents can't understand why they are crucified by the media when things go wrong and are all but ignored when things go right.

But in many, many cases, a school PR specialist could have done a lot more to assure fair, objective coverage of the school news. Controlling the press is out of the question. But working with them to assure accurate, objective coverage of both the good and the bad is what school-media relations should be all about.

After all, the news stories that appear in print will be no better than the information provided the reporter. The success a reporter has in telling your school story depends largely on your willingness to provide usable information, and how available you are to explain and clarify this information.

To be effective, the school PR specialist or school administrator must fully understand the media. He or she must be ready to accept the fact that, generally, bad news, rather than good, sells newspapers and determines the ratings of radio and TV newscasts. Certainly, features about kids and animals and some positive news are part of that package. But the simple fact is, that media that do not report violence, expose corruption, crusade for the taxpayer, hold a magnifying glass to the government fishbowl and tell where things went wrong usually go out of business.

Most people who buy newspapers and listen to the radio and watch TV expect the media to report what is going wrong. And they realize that without the media, Watergate might still just be an apartment complex in Washington, D.C.; Vietnam might still be underway in a rice paddy halfway around the world and Alexander Solzhenitsyn might still be a prisoner in a Russian jail.

Likewise, someone must keep a close watch on the tax dollar, be it spent for bombs or butter or the education of a child. And like it or not, education, as a major tax-consuming branch of government, is suspect by the taxpayers and by the media they support.

So it's up to the school board and the superintendent and the school PR specialist to allay that suspicion by running an open, honest, out-in-the-sunshine operation for all the world, including the media, to see.

Choose Your Battles

The school board that mistakenly wars with the media, even though sometimes it may be justified—because the media can have its slants, its prejudices, its vendettas, too—becomes the antagonist, the opponent of First Amendment rights, the government bureaucracy trying to impede this society's primary watchdog, the media.

School attorneys contemplating war with the media should remember the words of the anonymous sage who said he made it a practice never to fight with someone who bought ink by the barrels and paper by the ton.

It's a losing battle right from the start.

The answer, then, is to recognize the "givens" of working with the media—startling news sells newspapers and boosts broadcast ratings and positive news isn't startling—and work within this context for balanced coverage of school news.

For it is also another "given"—all too often overlooked by school districts—that most media, if treated frankly and honestly when test scores go down, or a teacher is assaulted, or a student is arrested for selling drugs, will reciprocate with positive coverage of a successful reading program, an outstanding science project, or a drive by students to provide food and clothing for the underprivileged.

That's not to say that the positive news necessarily will get the kind of banner headline, front-page treatment given to negative news, but it will be used. Conversely, when a school district blocks the news media from covering negative news, two things will happen: one, the media will get the negative news from someone, even if it's secondhand, inaccurate and blown out of proportion, and, too, you can forget about any coverage of positive news.

Try the Positive Approach

Yet, there need not be an adversarial relationship between the media and the schools. Most media people see their jobs exactly the same way educators see theirs: serving the community by educating it. And the easier educators make it for the media to do their job, the more balanced, or maybe even favorable, the coverage will be.

How To Complain

Yet, there is still another major responsibility. And that is knowing when and how to complain about unfair media coverage. Rich Bagin of the National School Public Relations Association offers this advice:

"You have a responsibility to let the media know when they've made a mistake. Take your complaint first to your reporter and point out the factual mistake. If factual errors continue, then it's time to alert the reporter's boss, the editor, of the continued inaccuracy through documentation. Now that may sound like a 'heavy' process, but remember you wouldn't fire a teacher just because a parent said the teacher was biased, so don't expect an editor to fire a reporter on your say-so.

"Most media people are after fair and accurate reporting and they'll see that you get it if your complaints are legitimate and you follow the proper channels. Don't complain because they ran that unflattering picture of you, or don't complain to a reporter about the headline that didn't have anything to do with the story because the reporters rarely have anything to do with headlines. Make your legitimate complaints factual and steer them to the right people and you'll see results if the paper's management is worth its salt."

Dealing With the Media

□ Respect the press as professionals and treat them accordingly. Most reporters today have to go through training similar to our teachers—four years of college and an internship to boot—so they deserve the same respect as all college graduates. You should treat them by the Golden Rule so professional relationships can blossom. That doesn't mean things will go the way you always want them to—far from it—but it does mean your relationship with the media will be on more solid ground which can be a bonus in a time of crisis.

□ Be available to speak on the issues. Perhaps the worst thing we can do is avoid or duck questions by conveniently not being available and stating "no comment." The "no comment" response only causes a reporter to think you are hiding something that could result in "bad press" for you and your district.

□ If you don't know the answer, say so, but promise to get back in 15 minutes or before deadline with an answer. By being conveniently absent when a reporter calls, you again start the reporter's juices flowing to unravel the scandal you must be hiding. And besides, the paper may just start an attack on why their $90,000 chief school administrator is always out of the office. Bad press, yes, and rightfully so.

□ Admit your mistakes when you make them. If something runs amuck—admit it—but

News Releases

The news release is the communications device most used by school districts. They are the easiest way to reach the media, but they are frequently not appreciated because they are, many times, poorly written, long-winded and contain little real news.

Anyone who ever worked for a newspaper knows that the person who winds up with 90 percent of the news releases a paper receives is the janitor, and he rarely has time to read them as he carries out the trash.

That's not to say that news releases can't be useful to both school districts and the media. Properly prepared and properly used they can be a great help to both.

First, the use: If you have an item of general interest to all your media outlets—like test scores, budget information, lunch and bus schedules, in the same breath explain what you're doing to rectify the problem. You'll be respected for that.

☐ Don't talk in gobbledygook and technical jargon. Speak and write in concrete terms and even provide a glossary of educational terms to all new reporters.

☐ Give out home phone numbers of top personnel designated to speak with the media.

☐ Encourage timely articles on long-range planning, assessment results, sex education, declining enrollments, teacher shortages, computer literacy so your district's positions are well understood.

☐ Encourage feature articles and photo features by providing potential material for the media.

☐ Maintain a file of updated biographies of all top administrators as well as mug shots of board members and coaches.

☐ Prepare background material for board meetings so that board action can clearly be understood.

☐ Alert reporters and photographers when cancellations occur.

☐ Periodically pick up the phone and tell a reporter that he or she did a good job.

☐ Learn what kind of photo assignments the papers will and will not run.

☐ Treat all media fairly; do not play favorites.

☐ Be honest, not secretive— what do you have to hide?

board meeting dates, kindergarten registration and the like—write a news release and send it out.

Such releases can be particularly helpful in interpreting test scores and budget information to the reporter who may not fully understand either process, and the use of information like bus schedules and kindergarten registrations dates are public service items that most media gladly accept.

Use your telephone as well. Select a particular media source like a newspaper that uses many photo features, or a TV station that likes an off-beat story now and then. Suggest to a reporter, person-to-person, that there might be a particularly interesting project at the science fair, or that awed children in a planetarium might make a good TV feature, or that the lefthanded biologist being honored is an interesting person with other redeeming qualifications that just might provide good interview possibilities.

When you have a good feature, like a graduate with 12 years perfect attendance, a parent with six children graduating from night school after 15 years, or a science class studying a six-foot boa constrictor, put that news release paper away and, again, pick up the telephone.

All your news outlets aren't going to rush over to interview the graduates or take pictures of the snake. With only a news release on a potential feature, you run the chance of having a potentially eyecatching story wind up as a two or three paragraph story under the truss ad on page 37. But a single paper or TV station, for instance, if contacted personally and promised the feature exclusively, just might play it up for all it's worth.

In other words, you've got to get the most out of each positive event, and a person-to-person approach is usually far superior to an impersonal piece of paper that has obviously been sent to every news outlet in town.

However, when news releases are used—and they are still necessary—here are some basic guidelines developed by Al Erxleben of the Florida Dept. of Education:

☐ Be sure you cover all the facts and are completely factual—don't editorialize.

☐ Simplify punctuation and hold it to a minimum.

☐ Always type your releases, double spaced, use 8-1/2 × 11 inch paper and use one side of the paper only.

☐ Always use the same format—same headings, same paragraph indentations, same margins. This helps to make your releases more professional and more recognizable.

☐ Do not hyphenate at the end of typewritten lines.

☐ Do not break a paragraph at the end of the page—and number all pages.

☐ Always adhere to the same spelling and capitalization style. You'll develop your own capitalization style and once you do, stick to it. Use a standard dictionary for spelling; here again, be consistent. When using the word "catalog," don't spell it one way one time and another way another time.

☐ Make sure the words in your release are spelled correctly—especially the names. And before distributing your news release to the media, proofread over and over, again and again.

Complete accuracy should be your goal. Typographical or editorial errors in spelling tend to make the facts—all the facts—in a news release suspect. If a well-known name is misspelled, how will the reporter who receives your news release know that you are being accurate when you say your school district spent $2,016.65 last year per student?

☐ Accuracy and speed are the hallmarks of the good information officer. Always make sure of your facts. Double check them, if you

have any doubts, but for heaven's sake, if you don't know, don't guess!
☐ Keep your releases timely. If your board meets at night, make sure the newspapers, radio and TV stations have a summary of board action the first thing the next morning. Stale news is no news.

Many districts design an attractive two-color eyecatching news-release sheet. This can be pre-printed and then typed on or duplicated. It provides quick identification of your information and builds awareness on the part of those covering the school beat. Be sure to include your office and home telephone numbers so that reporters can quickly locate you in time of need.

School Coverage

While some school public relations officers in smaller suburban districts may complain of not receiving enough publicity from the press, "big city" school officials often complain of too much coverage.

A former information specialist for the District of Columbia Public Schools worked with full-time education reporters from the city newspapers, television and radio stations. She reported that, "Urban assignment editors call you before they call neighboring school districts, simply because you're closer to the studio, and you're more likely to make page 1—especially when you don't want to!

"Editorial pages will be used to force school system policy. When there's bad news about the schools, the public is certain to attribute it to beleaguered city school districts. Conversely, good news about your schools is often attributed to counties whose schools are reputed to be good," she remarked.

Radio

As school districts concentrate their communication energies into vying for newspaper headlines and for a spot on the six o'clock TV news, far too often they ignore another extremely important communications medium—the radio.

And conversely, sometimes radio stations, especially the ones with 55 minutes of rock and five minutes of news straight off the radio wire, ignore local events.

Who needs them, you say? **You do.** Because as any parent of a teenager knows, the stations that feature "top of the chart" singers and groups are the stations that attract the major share of the student audience. And students, occasionally, contrary to popular opinion, do listen to the news.

If properly used, radio news reporters and program directors are a vital, if not key, link in telling the school story to your community, says William E. Henry of the Montgomery County (Md.) Public Schools. If misused, however, radio broadcasters can cause serious and often irreparable harm and damage to your credibility and image.

Henry offers these tips on the use of radio to tell the school district story:

☐ Use radio for emergency announcements concerning your school system (snow emergencies, early closings, late openings, etc.) Publicize widely in your community what station(s) will carry "official" school announcements and work out a code arrangement with station personnel to avoid crank calls.

☐ Spot announcements: utilize radio for 10-, 20-, 30-, or 60-second spot announcements concerning some particular aspect of your school district program (board of education meeting dates, holiday schedules, open house nights, dramatic and athletic events, honors programs, PTA meetings, etc.

☐ Vignette shows: use radio to highlight in short, punch broadcasts (preferably five minutes) concerning activities of the school district—such things as curriculum changes, explanations of board of education actions, the hiring of new personnel (especially new superintendents), new instructional programs.

☐ In-depth programs: once a month, half-hour public service productions devoted to an indepth analysis of the broad program activities of your school district (guidance counseling, vocational education, distributive education, office work experience, classes for the handicapped or gifted, etc.)

☐ Live board of education broadcasts: encourage a commercial station in your community, or the school radio station if you have one, to broadcast live sessions of board of education meetings so that your citizens will be able to hear first-hand the key decisions and deliberations of the board.

☐ Spot news: reaction, statements, explanations, or answers to key questions making news in your district and community.

Things to keep in mind when using (or increasing your use of) radio:

☐ Radio stations deal in seconds, and cannot use long statements and statements filled with "educationese" on the air. If you have a major announcement to make, issue a news release for the print media, but boil it down to the key ingredients (60 seconds or less) for use by radio.

☐ Remember that radio broadcasters (as all journalists) are generally trying to answer six key questions in any story they air. They are "Who, What, When, Where, Why and How." Make sure the Five Ws and the H are answered in all broadcast news releases.

☐ Get to know broadcast news reporters on a professional, first-name basis. Most news stories get distorted because of a lack of understanding by the news reporter, not by design.

☐ Don't attempt to mislead radio broadcasters concerning breaking news happenings in your school system. Give them the facts as you understand them, even if it is, in your opinion, a story which will not enhance the district's image.

The main ingredient, once again, is person-to-person contact. Don't assume a radio station isn't interested in school news and public service programming. And don't even ask on the telephone. Just call the station manager, make an appointment to see him or her, and sit down and talk about it. You may be surprised at the results.

Types of Radio-TV Programs

Before you contact the program director with a news feature idea, know the kinds of programs the station carries. Here are some of the possibilities:

☐ Specials: interviews, panel or group discussions and demonstrations as part of a series or as a one-time-only presentation.

☐ Segments: similar but shorter presentations inserted as "participating" features of other programs.

☐ Spots: brief announcements made at various times during the broadcast day.

☐ Personality spots: announcements by on-the-air personalities, such as disc jockeys or directors of women's features or farm programs.

☐ Editorials: statements which present the station's viewpoints on community programs or proposals. Some stations encourage responsible representatives of local groups to present opposing viewpoints.

Develop a few samples of possible programs from your schools, tape them on a cassette and play them at your interview. This shows the type of offering you are ready to produce, the quality of the material you can bring in, and that you have cared enough to do your homework.

CHAPTER ELEVEN

Handling the Basics

The five areas discussed in this section probably account for more of the school administrator's or professional school public relations expert's time than any other functions—excepting the production of district publications. They are at the core of what people want to know about and how they can be involved.

Advisory Committees

Schools are often a reflection of society, and education is everyone's responsibility. That, in effect, was one of the key concepts addressed by the National Commission on Excellence in Education in its *Nation at Risk* report. "Today, parents, non-parents, teachers, students, school board members, legislators and political leaders, the print and electronic media, military leaders, businesses, labor unions, and colleges and universities all have an important role to play," the Commission said.

What a change from earlier school days when the thought of citizens coming in to help a school district do a better job was an anathema to most boards of education around the country! Most boards ruled with an iron hand, few of them bothered to hear citizens at their monthly meetings. If someone dared suggest to a school board how to set policy for a school district, that person was viewed, more often than not, as a misinformed and misguided soul, at best, or, more likely, as some kind of radical troublemaker.

Today, after the educational reforms of the 1960s, and after federal legislation that mandated advisory committees as one criteria for federal aid to education, citizen advisory committees are recognized as necessary, and helpful, in most school systems throughout the country. Most school authorities have discovered they have at their disposal an abundant supply of public talent, time and willingness to work.

Citizens committees are now called into action for attacks not only on fiscal problems but on problems representing the entire range of school administration, instruction and community relations; some on an ad hoc basis, but many for continuing service.

Some of the questions a school district must ask before establishing a citizens' advisory committee or council should include:

☐ How do we set up a committee?

☐ How shall its members be named? What qualifications should they have? Will membership be representative of the community?

☐ If it is a continuing council or committee, how will membership be rotated?

☐ How do we get the most value from its work? Are there limitations to be placed on the committee? What kinds of tasks should a committee be asked to undertake?

☐ What are the characteristics of a committee which make the best contribution to a public school system?

☐ What funds will be necessary for committee business?

☐ Who will provide the leadership for the committee?

☐ What will be the specific charge (task) for the committee?

☐ When the committee has completed its work, what sort of reward is planned?

☐ Who is going to provide an evaluation of the committee?

There are hazards and dangers ahead when spurious reasons are advanced for the creation of committees and when these groups are misused in any of the following ways:

☐ **The committee as a rubber stamp.** When boards of education, or administrators, initiate questionable or controversial programs or policies, they often seek the support of a citizens committee. Rubber stamping an unsound idea seldom prevents future trouble.

☐ **The committee as shock absorber.** When attacks and criticism in a community rise and spread, some school authorities are tempted to create a citizens group to absorb some of the flak. Both the ethics and effectiveness of such a move can be questioned.

☐ **The committee as promoter.** When school authorities feel insecure in areas of budget, bond issues, curriculum change, student discipline or teacher negotiations, one natural tendency is to fall back on the committee as propagandizer.

☐ **The committee as bailer-out.** School boards in trouble with the community, teachers, students or taxpayers often create—in a hurry—citizens groups to save them. There is little evidence of successful outcomes in such instances.

There is a general agreement that school systems get in trouble because of poor school board policies or weak administration, and no citizens committee can correct these weaknesses. Nor can citizens committees come up with instant recommendations to get a faltering school system out of its sloughs of inefficiency. Only when organized for a sound purpose and only when nurtured with good care can the citizens group promote the cause of education in the community.

Sound purposes, one school board member has suggested, should include "agreeing on educational philosophy for the district, long-range planning, significant curriculum revision and instituting major organizational change." Also, when a school board gets involved in new concepts, such as open education, year-round schools or career education in the elementary schools, the citizens committee is a proper medium for helping the board get new insights, facts and concepts.

However, the board member warned, problems can occur if citizens committees go beyond their assigned advisory roles. "The cracks of failure," he warns, "begin to show in the districtwide committee when it becomes entangled with details of running a school."

Building Level Committees

Often the greatest benefit of advisory committees may be at the building level. School building administrators need advice on a large number of issues—from playground supervision to rules on smoking—and parents are frequently willing to give such advice. Building administrators also need workers for a large number of tasks, and again, citizens are usually willing to contribute their time and effort.

It is true that there can be problems associated with a citizens committee, such as guidelines for its operation and composition, the extent of its authority, what it should do and what it shouldn't do, how it should be dealt with if it tries to assume too much authority, its relationship with both the school board and the administration, and more.

The following sections provide practical, general guidelines for avoiding some of the pitfalls of citizens advisory committees and if followed, help insure a productive and cooperative working relationship between the committee and the school district.

Committee Composition

The membership of any committee depends, in part, on the function of the group. Some have six members, others 300. Most have 15 to 45 members. Some committees will require special expertise. Most general interest committees, however, strive to get a representative cross section of the district or of the neighborhood school. Criteria should include geographic location, income, ethnic background, religion, race and organizational affiliation.

The Upper St. Clair (Pa.) Township School District has used the following procedure for selecting advisory committee members that is both inclusive and representative of the community. A brochure is sent to residents explaining the purpose and limitations of district advisory committees. Residents are encouraged to mail in a perforated form to become part of the "membership bank." Any community resident, age 16 or older, is eligible. Returned cards are filed according to four age categories: 16-21, 22-44, 45-64, and 65 and older. Prospective advisors have the option of including their occupation and special interest or area of expertise. Those with special skills are coded with an "S" and their application is cross-referenced. When the school board creates a new committee or has a vacancy to fill, a drawing is held, using the appropriate age groups. The guidelines call for general committees to be composed of a cross section of township residents. About one-half of the membership chosen for a specialized committee has expertise in the topic to be studied.

In *The Open Partnership: Equality in Running the Schools,* author Charlotte Ryan describes the ideal committee as one that has both open and equal membership. Such a committee is open to students, teachers, parents, citizens and administrators—in short, any group that is likely to be affected by the decision. "Since change in institutions depends on change in individuals," Ryan writes, "it is important that all who will be affected by the decisions involved have an opportunity to share in making them, if change is to be effective." Equal membership, Ryan added, is a characteristic that is learned when people who are working together "come to appreciate each other's different perspectives and knowledge."

Guidelines for Advisory Committees

The kiss of death for a districtwide advisory committee is to create such a committee without a clear mandate. Even general committees should be given a specific task at the outset, so members do not feel they are wasting their time. Orientation and training are important, but they should not be allowed to become the sole purpose of the committee. In a study of advisory committees in a large countrywide school system, positive and negative comments were collected from committee members.

One of the negative comments, stated by a member of an area advisory committee, was, "Too much time (is) spent 'educating' us, instead of addressing major issues. By the time we are considered well informed enough to form an opinion, the year is over, frustrations are heightened, and a feeling of futility has set in."

Another trap to avoid is giving the committee members the impression they have more authority than they actually do. An *Education USA* survey asked school districts that use advisory committees to describe how much power or authority the committees have. Without exception, the committees were advisory only. This is not to say the committees are not influential.

To avoid pitfalls and to provide uniformity among advisory committees, many school boards have developed guidelines to govern the creation and operation of such committees. The Milwaukee (Wis.) Board of School Directors adopted comprehensive guidelines to govern board-initiated, administration-initiated and individual school-community advisory groups. As described by Milwaukee Supt. Lee McMurrin, the policies governing board-initiated committees state that:

☐ Board-initiated advisory committees will be districtwide in scope.
☐ Committee members will be advised at the outset that their powers are advisory.
☐ Members will be appointed by the school board president.
☐ Committee membership will ensure representation of the entire community.
☐ The committee will receive a letter of invitation stating the purpose and scope of the committee and the length of time each member is being asked to serve.
☐ The letter will either designate a chairperson or specify that the committee elect its own.
☐ The letter will specify the time and place of the first meeting, the dates on which reports are to be submitted, and the date by which the committee should complete its task.
☐ The superintendent or designee will serve the committee as a resource or liaison (any staff liaisons shall serve as non-voting members of the committee).
☐ Board members are encouraged to participate in advisory committees as non-voting and non-office holding members.
☐ A specific budget will be established if the duties of the committee require expenditures of money.
☐ All committee meetings are open to the public and a minimum of five days public notice should be given prior to each meeting.
☐ The superintendent and staff are expected to review and respond to committee recommendations presented to the board.
☐ After the board acts on the committee's report, the committee will be considered dissolved, and a letter recognizing the contributions of the committee will be sent to each member.

The key policies governing administration-initiated advisory groups in Milwaukee are that such groups should not compete with board-initiated or school-level committees, and that studies done by the committees and their recommendations should be reported to the board. If the committee includes employee groups, those representatives are to be selected by their bargaining unit. McMurrin said advisory groups created to comply with federal laws, like Chapter 1, should have a full-time staff member assigned to them.

The school-level advisory committee works under the guidance of the principal who is expected to work closely with the local PTA or PTO to organize the committee. The guidelines encourage representation by teachers, students, classified personnel, parents and other community members. Parents of children in the school are to comprise a majority of the committee. Each group that is represented should select its own members. In schools that have separate advisory committees for federal programs, like Head Start, the policies encourage these committees to be represented on the full school committees.

The committees are expected to meet at least four times a year, and to communicate with their constituents via newsletters and posters. The policies also establish a "chain of command" which the committees may use to gain additional information or to act upon a request. In Milwaukee, the chain is the local school principal, an administrative specialist at the district level, the superintendent and, ultimately, the board of school directors.

Here are some guidelines for local school councils from the publication *Schools Where Parents Make a Difference.*

   □ Decisions about size, membership, function and ways of working should be made by each school district through joint planning, involving the school committee, the superintendent, other central office administrators, teachers and teacher organizations, parents, citizens and students. Local conditions, needs, experience and values are the best guides for deciding what kind of council plan, if any, should be tried.

   □ Initiative can come from school people or community people. Regardless of who takes the first step, joint planning is essential from the beginning. A plan for collaboration developed unilaterally by administrators is not likely to succeed any better than a plan developed by a parent group without the genuine involvement of others who will be affected by the plan.

   □ Council members should be elected by a democratic process determined during planning. While a majority of the members should be parents of the children attending the school, councils should also include teachers and other school staff, community residents, nonparents and students. Even in elementary schools, the perspective of students—the "consumers" of the programs—can be helpful.

☐ Membership in the council should be representative of diverse groups and interests in the community, including different racial, cultural and economic backgrounds and different political or social viewpoints.

☐ Existing parent groups should play an important role in developing plans for a new council. It is important to coordinate such groups as parent-teacher-student associations (PTSAs), Chapter I or bilingual advisory committees. Having a school council does not eliminate the need for other groups. An existing PTSA, for example, can become an arm of a school council.

☐ A cooperative and mutually supportive relationship between the school council and the school principal is of special importance. The principal is in a key position to aid or block the development of an effective council.

☐ The members of a school council and the principal need assistance, information, orientation and planning for the council to have a fair chance of success. Lack of access to information about school policies, budgets and problems, and lack of training in organizing a group are the major causes of failure. Such support need not cost much money. But some financial support is necessary to cover the costs of planning, training workshops, duplication of materials and newsletters, and other means of communication with all members of the school community.

☐ The school board should see that each school council is evaluated at least once a year and that each council reports annually on its work, achievements and problems. The basis for such evaluation must be included in the original design of the council so standards for judging success are understood and agreed upon.

☐ An effective council needs written rules for its operation—developed jointly with and approved by the school board.

Evaluating the Committee

Two basic assumptions are essential to any successful school board advisory committee relationship. The first is that the committee's opinions will be respected and recommendations will be given serious consideration. The second assumption is that advisory committees have a right to receive an answer to their recommendations. The board should say which recommendations will be adopted. When recommendations are not adopted, the board should say why not for each one.

One pitfall to the use of advisory committees is that a school board can go overboard in creating advisory committees. When this happens, administrators become bogged down in filling committee requests for information. In such cases, the board may be abdicating its leadership responsibilities. To keep committees on the track and to guard against creating too much of a good thing, periodic evaluations of the committee structure can be helpful. A sample evaluation form is printed below. It is to be completed by committee members and the superintendent or staff liaison to the committee.

Citizen Advisory Committee Evaluation Form

☐ How well did the committee succeed in accomplishing its assignment?

☐ Did the committee seek help when needed?

☐ What were the difficulties experienced in actively involving all the members in the committee work?

☐ Did you feel that this committee was in conflict with any other school or community organization?

☐ In your opinion, are the guidelines for a citizen advisory committee clear and explicit?

☐ Was there strict adherence to the guidelines by all concerned? If not, why?

☐ Was there positive, two-way communication between the committee and the school district? If not, why?

☐ What were the total person-hours of certified staff?

☐ What were the strengths of the committee?

☐ What were the weaknesses of the committee?

☐ What could have been done to improve the committee's effectiveness?

☐ How can this evaluation format be improved?

The Curriculum

School districts—which previously spent much of their energy promoting "unique" or "innovative" programs in the print and broadcast media—have a golden opportunity to turn the public's attention toward the regular, basic core curriculum—a matter of vital importance to most parents.

Since *A Nation at Risk* was published, citizens across the country have been talking about and working to improve education. Local school boards have toughened education standards, putting academics at the head of the class. States like Texas, South Carolina, California and many others have pushed through major educational reform bills. Polls indicate that the public is concerned about the nation's educational system.

The axiom still holds true, despite the vast changes in public education during the past 20 years, that the very best public relations agent a school district can have is a student who goes home at the end of the day and says, "You know, I really learned something in school today."

But Ben Brodinsky, an educational public relations consultant and former school board member, explains, "The usual and ordinary things taking place in your classrooms form the best base for the public relations

List What You Want To Tell, Inform and Share

☐ **On the Elementary Level:**
Decide what you'd like to communicate about—reading instruction—mathematics—science—social studies—the arts! List other instructional areas. Be selective.

☐ **On the Secondary Level:**
What areas should you select for attention—language arts—science—math—social studies—the arts—vocational education—what about guidance and counseling?

What do you believe the people want to know?

☐ The results—student honors, achievements, test scores, etc.

☐ The content of the instructional areas

☐ The textbooks and instructional materials in use

☐ The methods applied

☐ Individualized approaches

☐ Independent study programs

☐ Use of cable television, computers, audiovisuals, field trips, resource people in the classroom

☐ What about the programs for special education? Talented and Gifted?

Decide on the media, the outlets, the channels you can use

☐ The weekly press

☐ Newsletters to parents

☐ Speeches by teachers and administrative staffs before local groups—count the local groups which may provide audiences (you may have more than you realize)

☐ The superintendent's annual report

☐ The special, one-shot leaflet or brochure

☐ Very brief leaflets on selected areas of the instructional program

☐ Radio or television spot announcements

☐ The open board of education meeting focusing on reading instruction, the pre-kindergarten program, etc.

of a local district. The continuing instructional program—for all students, by all teachers, in all areas of instruction—must be utilized on a continuing basis, for informational and public relations activities."

Brodinsky's advice:

In short, don't put all your PR eggs, or even most of them, in the media basket. Target your efforts. Select different ways to highlight programs at the district level and even more importantly, at the building level. Be proud of your basic curriculum. Promote it everywhere and anywhere you can. It's still the backbone of your school system and of your community relations.

School Board Meetings

Another area that cries out for better public relations in most school districts is the school board meeting.

It presents an ideal chance for school boards to communicate with parents and community leaders. Yet, in far too many cases, parents and community leaders go away mad; frustrated at not being listened to, angry at being treated brusquely, and appalled at listening to the board members fight among themselves while major issues go unresolved.

In the book, *PR For School Board Members,* the American Association of School Administrators says:

"The importance of the school board meeting as a communications vehicle should not be underestimated. It presents an excellent opportunity to improve relations with the community, and with the various publics—both external and internal—served by the board. Properly conducted, the board meeting offers board members a powerful and effective public relations device that goes a long way toward opening up true communications. Poorly conducted, the meeting can erode public support and undermine the overall public relations efforts of the district."

Nick Goble, assistant executive director for the Pennsylvania School Boards Association, puts it this way:

"There should be no surprises between board members and administration (at the meeting). Nothing can break down the business-like image of the board, crack its credibility, and sever its working relationship internally, like open criticism and confrontation at public meetings. Board members should not 'play' to the audience. Administrators should not allow the board to be caught in embarrassing situations. Through proper planning with the board president and the administrative team, the superintendent can prepare for the unexpected and, at the same time, set the stage for the board to conduct its affairs in an orderly fashion. Consequently, it is imperative that the administration maintain frank, open and continuing communications with the board. On the other hand, the board has a responsibility (through proper procedures) to inform the administration of citizen inquiries, complaints and concerns."

What Do the Meetings Say?

One of the easiest and most effective communications tools at the disposal of the school board is the board meeting itself. Rose M. Bullis, communications consultant at the University of Nevada-Reno, suggests that school districts ask themselves, "What do your school board meetings say about you?" She contends that the success of a school board meeting "is directly related to the advanced planning, the manner in which it is conducted, the extent of focus on students and curriculum, and the 'welcome' atmosphere in the board room."

Her suggestions for better public relations through better school board meetings are:

Plan Ahead

□ Information packets should contain comprehensive background information on each agenda item and should be distributed three or four days before the meeting. "Hand deliver" if necessary.

□ Distribute the agenda to key people in the community, the press, and staff members.

□ Make provision for people who wish to speak on an item on the agenda to call or write in order to ensure time on the agenda. Set the ground rules so that all speakers stay within a time limit.

Streamline the Meeting

□ Operate board meetings in a parliamentary fashion; and begin on time.

□ Presentations must be carefully prepared. Involve staff members in the presentation of as many items as possible in each board meeting.

□ Be sure everyone can see the visual presentations, hear what is being said, and receives a copy of handouts.

□ Do not overreact to criticism and never become defensive.

□ Follow statutes to the letter and hold executive sessions only when permitted by law (discussion of personnel matters, property acquisition, student discipline, security matters, or consultation with attorneys regarding litigation).

□ Publish a special bulletin covering the highlights of each board meeting and distribute to all staff members, key citizens and news media directors as soon as possible after the meeting. (The next day should be your goal.)

Focus on Students and Curriculum

□ Display student work at meetings. Consider having the flag salute led by a student, musical numbers or other student presentations at the opening of the meeting (5 to 10 minutes). Each meeting should include at least one presentation of interesting programs or teaching techniques by students and teachers (5 to 20 minutes). Recognize outstanding programs and practices in the schools, and have the staff responsible, at the meetings and introduce them publicly.

Humanize the Meeting

☐ Keep in mind that education is a people business.

☐ Greet people, hand them an agenda, and make them feel welcome.

☐ Have a coffee break.

☐ The board room should be easy to find and have adequate parking.

☐ Schedule meetings so they are convenient to the public. Try scheduling one meeting a month at 4 p.m. and one at 7 p.m.

☐ Invite special groups to attend board meetings or send representatives—Taxpayers Association, League of Women Voters, PTA Council, etc. Be sure they are introduced when they attend. Make them feel welcome.

☐ Provide an informational brochure for all visitors including names and/or pictures of board members, how they may participate in meetings and how to get additional information.

After the Meeting

☐ Have a district spokesperson available to meet with the press. Some school districts schedule a news conference with the superintendent and board president immediately after the meeting.

☐ Prepare a follow-up list of things to do as a result of comments, questions or suggestions offered at the meeting. Answer questions you promised to answer.

Going to the People

Many school boards are holding their meetings at various locations throughout the school district to provide board members and central office administrators an opportunity to listen to the concerns of a wider cross-section of citizens and give more citizens a chance to meet the board and to inform the community about the operation of their schools.

Here's how the Mobile County (Ala.) Public School System moved several of its meetings out into the community;

☐ Six meetings were set up in the urban and rural areas of the county. A 26-minute slide presentation was developed which detailed each of the six divisions of the school system—pupil personnel, business, general administration, personnel, curriculum and special services— and how all relate to the total operation of the schools. After the program was developed, a preview showing was held to give area leaders and members of the news media an opportunity to view the audiovisual presentation.

☐ To encourage parents and citizens to attend, news releases were sent out periodically and the two members of the community relations department made audio tapes for radio public service announcements.

☐ School board members as well as central office personnel attended each meeting. Persons attending were introduced to school officials and then shown the slide-tape presentation. Following this, parents were given an opportunity to ask questions. If they chose not to ask questions in the open meeting, they were invited to put their questions in writing and were promised written replies. Schools where meetings were held were responsible for after-meeting refreshments and general arrangements.

☐ Written questions from parents and interested persons were given to the public information office, which had the responsibility of researching answers and sending letters to the parents.

☐ Reception by the parents was very positive. About 80 percent of the responses received were most encouraging, with parents feeling that the meetings served a definite need and should be continued. Parents even suggested topics to be covered in other meetings, such as building program plans and curriculum.

The School District Budget

Perhaps no other single area causes a school district more concern than its annual budget.

And more often than not, it is not the budget itself that gets a school district into negative public relations with its community. It's the poor job many school officials do in explaining and interpreting their budget to the public that causes concern.

Tom Shannon, executive director of the National School Boards Association, contends:

> "The budget, with its potential for communicating the school district's approach to managing the educational enterprise, can be the foremost public relations tool in any district. The problem is that often it is not."

"The format of a school district budget," Shannon says, "must be developed "to tell most accurately and completely the budget story . . . to give a person who lacks expertise in school finance a good understanding of what the school board will spend his or her tax dollar for."

Shannon contends that far too many school systems are content to present their budgets in the "specific and detailed format prescribed by

Board Members Are 'PR' Persons, Too

Mike Torkelson, assistant executive director for the Minnesota School Boards Association, has the following public relations ideas for **individual school board members:**

□ Set board policy on public relations and communications and direct the superintendent to develop a program following this policy.

□ Visit your schools on a regular basis. Talk to students, teachers and other district employees.

□ Become a part of your school system's speakers bureau and be willing to talk to the community or student groups about schools and their operation—but do your homework first.

□ Appear on local television and radio interview shows.

□ Visit your local editor and leave both a personal picture and a biographical sketch for his or her use. For television stations, arrange for a slide picture of yourself to be in their files along with a biographical sketch.

□ Uninformed public? Conduct a series of informational sessions for district residents. Be honest, be prepared, be interesting.

□ Be informed and aware of accomplishments by your employees whether it be school related or otherwise.

state fiscal authorities. This format usually "bewilders even private accountants and bookkeepers, as well as businessmen, who have not had some exposure to the specialized application of government fiscal accounting to school district finance," Shannon notes.

Tell the School Story

"The official budget document presents a unique opportunity to tell your school story to the public," says Patty Farrell, community relations coordinator for the Reynolds Schools in Troutdale, Oregon. "In the past, budget documents in the Reynolds district had been a lifeless compilation of numbers, carrying almost no explanation. The budget committee was so frustrated that members began telling the community they didn't know what was in the budget!"

Farrell says the solution was a budget document that not only told the public where the money went, but also explained what it did when it got there. Two to four pages of explanation precedes each official program

Send them a congratulatory note.

□ Keep newspaper clippings of accomplishments by students. Send them and their parents a note.

□ Recognize the community contributions of citizens, especially those who have been involved in the schools. Send official letters of congratulations to each.

□ Keep in touch with your constituency—by telephone and written materials in addition to your personal contacts. If you have a "hot" issue, take a random sampling of opinion. People like to be asked their opinions.

□ Have someone develop a "welcome" brochure for visitors to school board meetings.

□ Circulate before and after meetings and introduce yourself to those you do not know and thank them for their interest and attendance—even if you didn't like what they had to say.

□ Take time to ride a school bus route or two during the year—you would be surprised at the rapport you can build up with bus drivers and students.

□ Make an effort to be visible at all school events—not just at football games.

□ Turn people on—be enthusiastic yourself.

entry in the document. In simple, plain English, these narratives contain the following elements:

□ Background of the specific program
□ Objectives of the program
□ Specifics outlining how the objectives are being met (description of what children are learning, the number of children served, the number of staff and their duties, and data on the effectiveness of the program)
□ Any proposed changes for the coming year

"Budget committee members appreciated the narratives," Farrell says, "and most took the time to read them. They then became better ambassadors for our schools because they knew more about what was taking place in the classrooms. In addition, school personnel finally had a document which explained the district's programs in detail. Tension and frustration were removed from budget meetings. Committee members were not embarrassed by being forced to ask simple questions about programs. Meetings were shorter and more productive."

Sharing Decisions

The Dallas (Texas) Independent School District has an elaborate, structured budget development process which seeks budget input from teachers, principals, students, parents and community groups.

The process began in the late 1960s as the Dallas school system set out to develop a goals program for the 1970s. It is still an important part of the budget development procedure in the 1980s as school officials try to hold down costs in the face of declining federal and state financial aid and rising costs.

Holding that quality education depended on effective, long-range planning, including needs assessment, priority setting and resource allocations, the Dallas school board asked the staff and the community at large to offer their ideas on objectives for the '70s.

What evolved was a "professional model for shared decision-making" in which priority goals were set, managers were appointed to develop specific objectives and program budgets, and both goals and objectives were adjusted from year to year to meet the changing needs of the schools, all with the participation of "literally thousands of Dallasites" during the past several years.

The first component of the model involved the setting up of a **District Communications Committee** (DCC), with every employee group in the school system represented. The DCC holds regular monthly meetings to make recommendations to the superintendent for action on school district matters, including the budget.

Another component is a **Dallas School Administrative Leadership Council** which meets regularly with the superintendent to provide rapid input on critical issues.

At the building level, each principal in the district's more than 200 schools has a **faculty advisory committee** composed of teachers selected by their peers to represent the views of the faculty.

In addition, an extensive leadership program for middle and high school students focuses young energies on school improvement and information efforts and develops members for **SUPER-SAC,** the Superintendent's Student Advisory Committee, which meets regularly with the superintendent to present the students' point of view.

Parents and other citizens are involved through the **Community Network,** which includes representatives from the business community; religious community; school-related organizations such as the PTA; youth agencies; realtors; institutions of higher education and private education; school "adopters;" community organizations and service clubs; district-wide advisory committees such as the **Hispanic Advisory Committee,** the **Native American Advisory Committee,** the **African American Ad-**

visory **Committee,** and the **Asian American Advisory Committee;** and key communicators such as senior citizens.

In addition, the superintendent meets regularly with school clusters of PTA officers, in various parts of the city and the **Positive Parents of Dallas,** a parent group which promotes and supports the school district.

School employees are involved through **Operation Involvement,** a systematic effort to assist the board of education in "assessing needs, assigning priorities and allocating resources as part of the annual budgeting process."

Operation Involvement members include representatives of each school elected by the faculty, principal representatives and central office staff. Each month the members meet in small discussion groups to focus on various areas of the school program. Employees are given released time for monthly sessions, which range from discussions on the latest school problem to field trips for background information.

Several times a year, representatives from each small group meet with the board of education to assist first-hand in setting program priorities. Each representative comes armed with input gained through extensive discussions at the individual school level. Representatives are given time at the local school faculty meeting to report on Operation Involvement activities and to poll teachers on their opinions.

Superintendent Linus Wright says there is little doubt that the Operation Involvement process has meant better decision making for the school system.

With a community and a staff as closely involved with all aspects of the school system as they are in Dallas, the support for school improvement projects like the $195.5 million bond issue approved in 1985, is built into the communication process.

The object of the process is credibility; credibility for education, for schools, for school personnel and for the children they serve.

The process itself is communication; communication with the many publics who are involved in a school system, internal and external publics alike. When that communication is frank and full and open and honest, the result is credibility.

And the result of credibility—particularly budget credibility—is the kind of community confidence without which a school district bond issue or tax levy doesn't stand a ghost of a chance.

Cutting the Budget

For decades school superintendents have heard the cry, "Taxes are too high," and school operating costs are "getting out of hand." Yet, in most school districts the public has, either grudgingly or willingly, come up with the dollars necessary to operate the schools.

In fact, most surveys since the *Nation at Risk* report seem to indicate that citizens would be willing to pay increased taxes to improve academic achievement in the schools. Most seem to think teachers should be paid more, too.

Yet, school districts still face the problem of declining enrollments and increasing costs. In past years school officials could point out that enrollment was climbing, necessitating more teachers and more facilities. But today, because of declining enrollment, the schools have fewer "clients." The common public cry now is "How can it cost more to educate fewer?"

Here are suggestions from the Mt. Lebanon School District in Pittsburgh, Pa., which provide some help in explaining this paradox:
□ Capital outlays (what you've done without)
□ Energy reduction efforts
□ Staff reductions (not just salaries, but fringe benefits, too)
□ Reductions in clerical and custodial services
□ Charges for consumable materials and field trip expenses previously provided free
□ Increased tuition for summer school
□ Reduction or elimination of courses with marginal interest
□ Permitting class sizes to rise
□ Closing or consolidation of school facilities
□ Increased charges for outside groups using school facilities
□ And any other items on which you have made savings.
Explain your budget clearly—particularly those expenditures which are for all practical purposes "uncontrollable."
□ Debit service on existing bonds, equipment, etc.
□ Negotiated salaries
□ Basic utility costs
□ Insurance rates
□ Effects of inflation on the purchasing power of the school district dollar
□ Costs of special programs mandated by state or federal government, such as compensatory education, education for the handicapped, etc.

Public School Vouchers

Public school vouchers are suggested by President Reagan as a promising way to improve elementary and secondary education in the United States. This attention comes at a time when proponents of tuition tax credits for private schools concede little chance for their proposals to pass Congress. Scott D. Thomson, executive director of the National Association of Secondary School Principals, believes public school vouchers are viewed as more acceptable on Capitol Hill by advocates of "family choice" in schooling.

"As a political strategy to break the nation's commitment to traditional public school finance, the voucher on the surface looks promising," Thomson wrote in *The Christian Science Monitor.* "But proponents vastly oversimplify the funneling of dollars to educate individual students and they ignore the erosion of public control over schools under a voucher system."

Thomson says a special formula would be necessary under a voucher system to pay the expense of special education students. Also, there is a range of costs of regular students which few people understand.

"The most rational financial system is one that takes the sum of resources available for schools in a community and directs them in the fairest way possible to all students in the community," Thomson says. "The traditional approach to school finance is the most flexible, the least bureaucratic, and the most beneficial in the long run. Services to individual students flow from the sum of resources available for all students."

Even more critical, Thomson believes, is that community control of school policy would be eroded. "Under a voucher plan, parents would gain power, since the vouchers would become theirs to spend. The general citizenry, however, would become disenfranchised, because policy would be determined by private expenditure. It would be the ultimate example of private consumerism at public expense."

Thomson concludes: "Public school vouchers appeal at first glance. But if the public's general interest in developing brain power for the future growth of the nation is legitimate, along with a parent's particular interest in a child, then the power to make educational policy must be shared. And if we want a new engine to improve schooling, let us first avoid installing an old and defective part."

Bond Issues and Tax Levies

Whether it is a school board election, bond issue, finance referendum or tax initiative which will directly affect schools, elections in the 1980s and beyond will no longer be won or lost with the votes of parents whose children attend the schools. The decision will rest with a growing majority of voters called "non-parents."

This non-parent group will decide whether school bonds are approved, whether needed funds are provided or whether restrictive tax initiatives will be mandated. And this group of critical voters will continue to expand in proportion to voters who are parents of children in public schools in the decade ahead.

The foundation of almost every successful finance campaign studied by NSPRA for its "You Can Win At The Polls" campaign kit, is an ongoing, well-developed and organized year-round public relations program. In a few cases issues are passed without such a PR program in place, but even in these cases, the campaign effort resulted in the establishment of an ongoing public relations program after the election.

It has been shown repeatedly that the success or failure of school finance campaigns is frequently determined even before the first announcement of an election is made.

Voters cast their ballots based on their attitudes about schools. They are also greatly influenced by their friends. These attitudes are a by-product of the experiences they may have had with their schools, school employees, students and even stories they have heard from sources they trust.

A great many people, still the majority in many communities, have moderate to strongly positive attitudes about their schools. In a finance campaign, schools must work to maintain and even intensify the positive attitudes of this group.

Another large group of people in most communities is "on the fence"—the undecided—in their attitudes toward their schools. Their attitudes are neither strongly positive nor negative. Your effort needs to be designed to convert this group to positive attitudes and votes.

A smaller but very important group in any community is made up of those with moderate to strongly negative school attitudes. Their attitudes have taken years to form and will not easily be changed. Your job will be to neutralize the negative effort of these potential "no" voters.

School operating levies, bond issues, the school budget in some areas, and tax initiatives like Proposition #13 in California, provide some of the last remaining opportunities for voters to cast their ballot for or against taxes of any kind. A voter pushing the lever of a machine, marking a paper ballot, or punching out his or her vote on a card may be voting for or against a myriad of issues and frustrations the very least of which is the actual school finance campaign. The result can be awesome as it determines the very future of the nation itself through the contribution each vote makes to the preservation of the public schools or their demise.

Executive Director John H. Wherry of the National School Public Relations Association says studies show that those with a great deal of confidence generally want to spend more on education—and so do a very large percentage of those who say they have hardly any confidence!

"Even those who don't have confidence in educators still want to spend more on education," Wherry says. "Apparently this is in the hope of straightening it out." But the point Wherry makes is that the majority of the public clearly think education is very important and are willing to provide the funds to support it.

Different Strategies Needed

As in successful PR programs where there are "different strokes for different folks (publics)," so in school finance elections there is a need for "different election strategies for different elections." Some suggestions may work well in some areas, but will be ill-suited for another.

Each election must be individually designed to suit the unique needs of the district and community in which it is being conducted.

J. William Jones, director of information services for the School District of Philadelphia, Pa., and author of NSPRA's book, *Budget/Finance Campaigns—You Can't Afford to Lose,* wrote in that publication, "For while no one campaign blueprint works everywhere, there are certain definite components to almost every successful school finance election, be it in a big city, in a small town or in any of the thousands of school districts in between.

"These components don't fall together by chance. They are the products of a carefully planned political process, the results of the nitty gritty of campaign policies, of asking yourself every conceivable question and coming up with answers to match, of understanding the dynamics of successful electioneering and applying them throughout the school district through the sweat and toil of a dedicated, volunteer campaign team."

Ten Steps to Success

In studying more than 50 successful school district elections in recent years the National School Public Relations Association found that although campaign strategies vary with local districts and regions, all successful efforts appear to have 10 basic and strategic steps:

1. **A strong public relations program.** The vast majority of successful elections are built on the foundation of a strong, ongoing, well-developed and organized, year-round public relations program. All is not lost, however, if a district facing a finance election does not have a formal public

relations program in place. Every district presently has a number of activities between the school district and the community whether formally identified as a "PR program" or not. For those districts without a formally structured PR program, a district finance election can well provide a golden opportunity to establish one.

2. **Pre-plan/study and analyze.** The question most frequently asked about school elections, whether bond issue or finance, is "how long a time line do we need for the election? The answer is "as much as possible." Obviously, the longer the planning period the more opportunity there is for a thorough study of the issue by key district publics and analysis of the proposal to be placed before the voters. The election time line covers not only that critical period which takes place prior to any announcement of an election and before the board of education decision is made to hold an election, but also that period after the announcement is made through the campaign and even after the election itself.

3. **Study district historical data.** Successful campaign specialists across the nation consider the maintenance of post-election materials the most critical part of any election. The compilation of election results precinct-by-precinct, evaluation of what worked and what didn't work in the election campaign, and a summary of election procedures serve as the framework for succeeding elections. Occasionally, however, a district will find itself going for a school finance election with little or no current historical election data. It is suggested that such districts study the results of other elections in their communities such as those for libraries or municipal services as a general guide, but avoid using as criteria election results where political party voters were involved.

4. **Survey your community.** Another key element in the pre-planning period for an election is an assessment of the community's attitudes about its schools. At what stage in the pre-planning process such a survey should be undertaken varies from district to district. But in view of the rapidity with which voting patterns change, it appears critical that any such survey be conducted within the 12 months preceding an election.

5. **Develop election campaign strategy.** It is vital that all be in order for the first announcement when the board of education takes formal action on the proposal to hold an election. Too much importance cannot be placed on having a unanimous board decision on any school finance election proposal. A split board alerts the community that something "isn't right" and that is all some need to vote "no" or stay away from the polls. In the election announcement, it is the responsibility of school administrators and their communication specialists to present the proposal in simple, clear, easily understood terms.

6. **Conduct a special voter registration.** This effort will emphasize the importance the district places on community involvement in the schools. It provides additional media coverage and an opportunity to bring non-

Tell the total staff as quickly as possible following the board decision to hold an election. The majority of districts with successful
bond election efforts indicate that an election chairperson(s) was
appointed by the school board or a "committee to support the election" was organized as a separate citizens effort. Many school districts call a news conference for the media to announce a proposed
election. It is essential that a school district administrator serve as
election coordinator or liaison to the steering committee to coordinate all groups and efforts.

registered people into the schools. Special voter registrations can also
mean the difference between winning or losing an election.

7. **Develop targeted election materials.** These materials must be carefully evaluated by each district and/or neighborhood to determine those
best suited to meet specific needs of their particular community. Those
districts requiring a super-majority vote will need to develop far more
materials than those requiring a simple majority, and if the election is to
be won they will have to target their interpersonal efforts in the closing
day of the campaign to those people previously identified as **positive
voters.**

8. **Identify "yes" vote and plurality needed for victory.** In the study
of winning elections, a strategy long part of political campaigns surfaces
as the pivotal element in school finance campaigns nationwide. It is the
political analysis technique based on a study of the district's past-election
results, precinct-by-precinct; the establishment of the maximum number
of "yes" votes needed to secure passage; identification of those precincts
most likely to produce favorable votes; and, a system to reach these voters
and get them to the polls on election day. **It is this strategy which the
winners credit with their election victories.**

9. **Plan election day strategy.** This is the day when nothing can be left
to chance. Winning districts build their election strategy to peak on
election day. Checklists for campaign workers generally include procedures for each building principal to make sure the election poll in his or
her building is open and ready to go at the start of election hours. Plan
to hold coffees in the school for early voters. Have plans, including
scripts, ready for telephone canvassers to go into action with last-minute
reminder calls to identified "yes" voters. Study the election turn-out to
identify whether heavy or light and have plans ready to go into operation
to turn out the vote if action is needed. Have babysitters and transportation available. Send home election reminders with students and establish an election watch center. Develop plans to announce election results

as quickly as possible and provide a press room for reporters covering the election.

10. **Debriefing and evaluation/the end . . . the beginning.** The election does not end until the final step—evaluation and compilation of election data—is taken. This is the pulling together of the entire campaign into an historical record. Most districts compile this material into a loose-leaf notebook ready to review for the next election. It should include every piece of material sent out and an analysis or summary written by the election coordinator of his or her impression of the election: what worked; what didn't; what should be dropped from future election campaigns; what should be included. A post-election survey submitted to a random sample of district voters can also provide valuable historic data.

CHAPTER TWELVE

Dealing with
Special Problems

One thing is certain. All school systems have problems. There are hundreds, perhaps thousands of different kinds, and they vary in size and intensity. But they are definitely there. And the school district that pretends they aren't is in trouble with its community already.

Whereas many districts have comprehensive PR programs-it is becoming evident that additional attention needs to be given to special problems that create community and/or staff concerns. These areas are the focus of this chapter—staff morale, discipline, violence, vandalism, closing schools, releasing test scores, strikes and desegregation. The PR models developed for these critical eight can serve a district well in handling the next ones that come along.

Staff Morale

Declines in enrollment and teacher lay-offs . . . competency testing . . . paperwork . . . low salaries . . . criticism by the public and press . . . the burden of maintaining discipline in the classroom . . . it's no wonder that many teachers and school staff members are depressed, exhausted and burned out.

There is perhaps no public relations problem more consistent or more elusive than low staff morale. The "them against us" mentality often separating staff and administration feeds the morale problem with a steady diet of distrust and negative thinking. Administrative programs aimed at addressing the problem have frequently been rejected by staff as "putting a Band-aid on a broken leg." These attempts have died quiet or noisy deaths depending on the level of frustration experienced.

But burnout is real, and can result in everything from worry to chronic migraines and ulcers. According to the NSPRA packet, "Lighting the

Fire—A Process for Building Staff Morale and Excellence," burnout stems from seven specific causes:
1. Lack of recognition,
2. Lack of involvement,
3. Chronic discipline problems,
4. Lack of planning time,
5. Media assault,
6. Public scrutiny and
7. Less turnover in teaching staffs.

The Cost of Burnout and Stress

In business the cost of stress-induced dysfunction in financial terms is staggering. The annual loss of productive capacity is reaching estimates of $19 billion and stress-related illness is estimated at $60 billion, according to a study by the University of Pittsburgh (Pa.) Graduate School of Public and International Affairs.

In education the cost is higher when it is translated into the loss of tomorrow's outstanding leaders and to individual teachers, principals and administrators in whom burnout symptoms limit not only their present productivity, but their future, even if they change careers.

Add to that the boys and girls who can lose an entire year of schooling because of poor teaching and classroom tension and you have a loss to which you cannot even assign a dollar figure.

As today's educators and their staffs reel from reports of mediocrity and calls for education reform; as staff members and boards of education confront one another across negotiation tables; as governors and legislators adopt new educational reform measures calling for teacher testing programs, competency examinations, merit pay proposals and more time on task, the stress level rises. It creates a climate of stress.

According to the "Lighting the Fire" booklet, "Self-motivation is the key to building staff morale and excellence." A person cannot be motivated until he or she reflects on the reasons for the need to be renewed. These include:
- ☐ Maintaining, regaining/renewing personal and professional energy,
- ☐ Being able to look at your own situation and gain awareness about it,
- ☐ Being able to talk to people who are in the same situation, people with whom you can share your concerns,
- ☐ Being able to focus on the positive rather than the negative,
- ☐ Being able to look at new and old problems in more creative ways to seek solutions,
- ☐ Being able to set goals, make plans and decide what's really important and what is not,

☐ Increasing your skills in dealing with other people,

☐ Being able to focus on the present rather than blaming past mistakes for current problems and

☐ Being able to prioritize problems and turn them into "opportunities."

Communication Is a Key

In order for any staff renewal efforts to be effective, administrators, principals and other leaders must be in contact with their staffs in both formal and informal settings. Opportunities to socialize together and interpersonal communication are essential factors for they **build trust.** Communication—effective two-way communication—has been shown to both motivate a staff, build needed trust and reduce burnout and stress.

Building Morale

Employee morale is founded on a feeling of self-worth, recognition for a job well done, comfort with evaluation methods and a feeling of being included in deciding how his or her work is to be performed or changed according to research studies. To ignore this is to create a climate of stress.

A study conducted by George Mason University of employees' responses to "What they wanted from their jobs," and management's conception of "what they wanted" points out a striking misconception on the part of management. First on the list from workers was for "full appreciation for work done." While first on management's list was "good wages."

Staff Renewal: Successful Approaches

Successful businesses and schools have identified a number of approaches to staff renewal which are producing excellent results. One of the newest and one making a rapid transition from business to schools, is that of Quality Circles. These ongoing teams of from eight to 10 members of an organization (staff) meet voluntarily on a regular basis to participate in the improvement of the organization. The concept springs from the work of Dr. Walter Demming of Harvard University, Cambridge, Mass., who helped bring about the radical changes in Japanese industry in the 1950s.

The health and wellness approach adopted by the suburban Minneapolis school district of St. Louis Park (Minn.) offers a successful school-based model for staff renewal. In the spring of 1980 the superintendent

What Do Workers Want from Their Jobs?

	Employees Rank	Management Rank
Good working conditions	9	4
Feeling "in" on things	2	10
Tactful disciplining	10	7
Full appreciation for work done	1	8
Management loyalty to workers	8	6
Good wages	5	1
Promotion and growth with company	7	3
Sympathetic understanding of personal problems	3	9
Job security	4	2
Interesting work	6	5

appointed a committee of interested staff volunteers to work during the 1980-81 school year to develop a "wellness program" for district employees. This committee included both professional and support staff members. The school board demonstrated its support and commitment to the project by designating $10,000 to be used to develop the program.

The results were exciting. A "Wellness" newsletter was developed, athletic programs were established along with aerobic classes, special workshops on coping with stress, developing hobbies, and planning for retirement were introduced. Individual schools purchased equipment to help staff members work off tensions including a standing bicycle that had over 3,000 miles registered in one week and two punching bags!

Quality Circles and Wellness Programs are not the only approaches that school districts have taken in building staff morale. There are a number of other approaches which have produced excellent results. These include:

- **Project Lightbulb**—a program of mini-grants to encourage teacher creativity.
- **Super Secretaries Sell Schools**—a long-range, inservice program to build professionalism.
- **Finding the New in You**—a project to provide opportunities for all staff members to explore new jobs.
- **Administrative Leadership Academy**—providing a management program based on a self-assessment approach for central and building-level administrators.
- **What's a Wheel Without Spokes?**—an inservice training program for custodians on issues affecting the educational system.

- **Breakfast Forums**—meetings of staff members with the superintendent on a weekly basis for open-ended, free-wheeling discussions.
- **Your Personal Interest Makes the Difference**—making a bridge between management and staff through personal relationships established in a professional way.
- **Food for Thought**—local observances for National School Lunch Week to bring recognition to the food service staff.
- **The Fourth "R"**—Recognition program designed to bring community recognition to schools and their staff members.

Discipline

Perhaps, year in and year out, there is no greater problem than discipline in the classrooms of America. Just about every year, people across the country tell the annual Gallup Poll of Public Attitudes Toward Public Education that discipline is their foremost concern.

Teachers and administrators wring their hands over the problem of discipline in cities and suburbia alike. Long thought to be a "city" problem, discipline, or the lack of it, transcends classes, races, and geography.

So what do you do? How do you involve the public and assure them that steps are being taken to overcome the problem? How do you admit the problem and begin to deal with it before the community demands that you do? And how do you involve them in the solution?

Perceptions Count

When we talk about "the school discipline problem," we need to define what we mean. We are talking about student behavior that disrupts the learning environment. There have always been some discipline problems in the schools, but as society changes more demands are put on young people. This can lead to stress, frustration, anger—and problems.

Changes like the lower drinking age, increased availability and use of illegal drugs, more single parent families, more moving from place to place have a powerful impact on young persons.

One thing is certain—there is no single cause of school discipline problems and there's no simple solution. It takes a team effort on the part of the schools, parents, churches and the community to effectively deal with the problem of discipline.

The Philadelphia (Pa.) Schools have put together a 69-page, working document used by the board of education, school district staff, parents, students and community groups to forge new school discipline codes.

Here's what some schools are doing about the discipline problem:
- ☐ Providing trained counselors and advisors for students.
- ☐ Giving teachers extra training.
- ☐ Trying to make course offerings as interesting as possible.
- ☐ Trying different types of approaches—like the "back to the basics" and other alternative schools.
- ☐ Developing a student "code of conduct" that spells out school rules and provides a discipline "contract" that the student, parents, teacher and principal sign and agree to follow.

The document, "Discipline in the Philadelphia Schools," is a compilation, under a single cover, of all the many existing school district discipline policies and procedures. Some dated back more than 20 years. Never before had they all been compiled in one place.

The discipline document was geared:
- ☐ To retain and re-emphasize sound principles of good teaching and good control;
- ☐ To place all disciplinary policies and guidelines in one convenient reference source;
- ☐ To provide suggestions for dealing with all types of disruptive behavior confronting the total staff in schools today;
- ☐ To suggest strategies for dealing with the overall problem of discipline in schools with respect to the changing parameters in which staff must function;
- ☐ To re-emphasize the need for shared commitment and responsibility by all who have a role to play in education in schools.

The school superintendent noted that in an urban school system like Philadelphia, different schools have different problems. Different staffs and parents and communities may want to pursue discipline in different ways. The object was to get everyone thinking, planning and implementing discipline.

The school district noted that the problems of violence and disruption are people problems. Their causes are deep-rooted and stem from many sources both within and outside of the school. The long-range solution to these problems, it said, will require personnel who have developed the skills and strategies to identify and remedy the causes of disruption.

"The School District of Philadelphia is committed to the goal of safe schools and an orderly process of instruction," it said. "This commitment requires that everyone, members of the board of education, central office personnel, school administrator, teacher, parent and student, assumes his or her share of responsibility toward the attainment of that goal. To do otherwise would be a great disservice to the young people of our community."

The moral of this story: if you have a discipline problem in your school and if the community is concerned about it, involve everyone in the solution—students, staff, parents and community members.

Here's a checklist of things parents can do to reduce discipline problems of their own children:

☐ Set realistic goals with your child—don't expect too much—or too little.

☐ Reward good behavior, don't concentrate on just punishing the bad. But remember, too much of either reward or punishment can cause problems.

☐ Take an interest in all aspects of your child's life—both in and out of school. Get to know the child!

☐ Be consistent and realistic about rules.

☐ Accept some of the responsibility for your child's behavior. In many ways your child is a reflection of you.

Violence

The need for better defined codes of discipline in the nation's schools is an end result. One of the prime causes is an alarming increase of violence in the classroom. Surveys in recent years have shown increases in school-related homicides, robberies, rapes and attempted rapes, assaults on students and teachers, burglaries, drug and alcohol offenses on school property, dropouts and in the number of weapons confiscated by school authorities.

Yet, too many school and even college and university executives seem to think that violence is something that can't or won't happen to them. And if it does, the answer too often is a mad dash for security guards, metal detectors and mass suspensions.

It is time to look at the PR implications of school violence, to admit that it can happen in any school system and start thinking "negatively" in order to do something "positively" about it. That's the advice of Robert Hilldrup, a former teacher, education editor and columnist, writing in the *Journal of Educational Communications*. Hilldrup says you have to expect the problem and plan to meet it head on.

One of the first aspects of the planning process, Hilldrup says, is to talk with the police. "This," he says, "is a badly overlooked area. Don't be too proud to talk to the cops. They don't want to take over education. They have enough problems. But they are willing to help. They will make security checks of school buildings to point out unsafe areas. They probably know a good bit about who is pushing or using hard or soft drugs and where. Get their advice. Establish communication with them before the needs of crisis arrive. Have a high ranking contact in the police department so you can decide who will make what statement to whom after an incident happens."

Next, Hilldrup says, move quickly to involve appropriate parent groups and establish ground rules with the news media.

His advice for dealing with parents:

> "The boards or executive committees of districtwide parents' organizations should be kept informed about your contingency plans. Principals, in messages to parents, should stress parental responsibility for attitudes and actions by pupils. Suspension and expulsion rules should be reviewed for conformance with the latest court decisions and parents and students should be informed of these."

There must also be guidelines for dealing with the news media in times of violence in the schools. Here are some suggestions:

- ☐ An incident in a school will probably involve a violation of law. The police are in charge of crime scenes and crime sites. Statements involving evidence or potential testimony should be cleared through the police. Photographers should not be allowed on a crime scene without prior police agreement.
- ☐ School employees should be told that if they have knowledge of an incident they do not have to make a statement **to the media** unless they wish to do so.
- ☐ A board policy should specify that reporters are not allowed to interview pupils on school property about an incident. Conversely, you cannot interfere with news media attempts to interview anyone, pupil or otherwise, once they have left the school building and ground.

With this kind of pre-planning and board policy in place, a violent act in the schools should not come as an indictment of your school or system.

Vandalism

As violence is primarily a problem during the day, so is vandalism primarily at night.

Vandalism itself costs school districts across the country millions of dollars a year. Related activities, like burglary and fire, mushroom the figure even more.

Broken windows in schools have become an epidemic. Vandalism damage includes flag poles and computers, toilets and turf, thermostats and fountainspouts; in short, just about anything connected with a school.

Yet, here again there are answers. **It is community involvement.** There is little argument anymore that one of the keys to an effective campaign on the mounting losses incurred by schools in the rising tide of vandalism is the development of a good working relationship with the community.

At the very least, everyone in the school and the community should be made aware of what vandalism costs in decreasing faith in the educational system, increasing costs for repairs and security measures, and the corresponding decrease in available funds for necessary education programs.

But more than awareness is needed to combat vandalism. And, again, proper planning and involvement is the answer; planning which involves staff, students, parents, community leaders and law enforcement agencies.

School districts across the country report the following steps in successful anti-vandalism campaigns:

- ☐ **Analyze and define the problem.** The first step must be the development of sufficient data to define the problem. This means a specific district policy on reporting ALL incidents.
- ☐ **Establish a clearly defined district policy** for reporting incidents complete with a standard form. Such a policy will provide accurate information, and is of immeasurable help in explaining what actually occurred. And after the policy is developed with the aid of administrators, support staff teachers and the school board, make sure it is disseminated to all personnel in the district.
- ☐ **Let the community IN on your concerns.** Establish either a school- or districtwide citizens advisory committee to work with you in developing plans, programs and policies that will help to reduce or eliminate the problem.
- ☐ **Encourage parents to talk with their children** about the effects of vandalism on their education. And encourage parents to notify the school of rumors or threats of vandalism or violence that their children report to them.
- ☐ **Establish a policy** in which parents become financially responsible for the damage to school property which their children may do.
- ☐ **Establish a good working relationship** with the local law enforcement agencies.
- ☐ **Institute a neighborhood watch system.** Enlist the aid of the school's neighbors in reporting all suspicious movements around school grounds as soon as they are noted. Try to guarantee anonymity to ensure more cooperation.
- ☐ **Form a parent patrol,** with school property marked with signs reading "This school is protected by community residents and the parent patrol." Under this plan, parents are encouraged to drive slowly by and around the school grounds during time periods (nights, weekends, vacations) when the premises are ordinarily unoccupied.
- ☐ **Establish a special number** which community members can call when they spot suspicious activity around a school.
- ☐ **Hold a series of informal briefings** with community residents on the school's problems and ask them for suggestions.

Closing Schools

Back in the 1960s, students were hanging out the windows, a broom closet with any size at all was used as a classroom, school officials were planning all kinds of new educational facilities, and it seemed the baby boom would never end.

But what a difference a few years makes.

Along came "the pill" and then tight money and unemployment and inflation, and by the early 1970s the baby boom was over. By the mid-'70s, school boards were laying off teachers, watching state subsidies fade away, and working to close down low enrollment neighborhood schools.

Unfortunately, some districts were closing the schools, or attempting to, more often than not, without proper planning, communication, or community involvement.

Yet, other districts, which acted on a logical plan communicated that plan to the community, and involved them in decision making closed schools and continued their reserve of goodwill.

In its publication, *Fewer Pupils/Surplus Space,* the Educational Facilities Laboratories (EFL) presents a plan, which has been used successfully by many school districts throughout the country. It contains five essential steps in reaching a justifiable decision on how to deal with enrollment declines:

1. A set of agreed-on goals, with specific objectives for each.
2. A factual base defining the "givens" upon which the plan can be developed. In the case of a plan for facility use, this base includes

---

Closing a school would mean:

- ☐ Keeping students relatively close to their neighborhood.
- ☐ Keeping students from crossing major physical barriers.
- ☐ Maintaining a similar socioeconomic, racial and ethnic mix.
- ☐ Closing the school with the lowest enrollment.
- ☐ Closing the oldest school with the weakest academic performance record.
- ☐ Closing the least educationally flexible building.
- ☐ Closing the "high-cost" maintenance/capital outlay building.
- ☐ Closing a building that can be recycled.
- ☐ Closing the building that requires the least additional cost in districtwide transportation.
- ☐ Closing the building most in keeping with the recommendations of the district's task force on declining enrollment.

Nostalgia Night

Here's how the school board in the Butler (Pa.) Area Schools countered community resentment a few years ago at the planned closing of the old Broad Street School with a "Nostalgia Night."

First, the faculty and staff of the school were involved in choosing a suitable date in late May. Through news releases, the community was asked to contribute pictures and other mementos for a display. Retired teachers, through their organization, were invited to participate, particularly those who had taught at Broad Street.

The PTA agreed to supply refreshments for the evening, and the children began making decorations. Even the mayor and city council cooperated by declaring the last week in May as "Broad Street School Week." Downtown merchants supported the project by running a Nostalgia Night logo in their ads.

Finally, May 28 arrived. The display of pictures was impressive, the building was decorated, the refreshments were ready, and the weather was perfect. But would the community come? The whole idea, after all, had really been a gamble.

The response was overwhelming. According to officials, more than 500 people of all ages jammed the small elementary school. They came by bus, car, cab and on foot. Many carried their old report cards and pictures with them to share with friends. PTA members ran out of refreshments and rushed out for more. People were reluctant to leave and sat for hours exchanging memories.

Opposition to demolition of the school literally ended that evening. Nostalgia Night allowed people to focus on their nostalgia.

It was a combination community block party and old-fashioned family reunion. The people who contributed to the displays and otherwise helped make Nostalgia Night such a tremendous success received special letters of invitation to attend Open House at the **New Broad Street School** in the fall.

enrollments and their projections; schools, their location, capacity and general level of adequacy; community changes affecting the location of people and the composition of their groupings; and a "picture" of the physical structure of the district. Cost data on new construction and/or renovation may also be required.

3. An analysis of the factual data. This is an exercise in fitting the numbers—pupils and schools—together and of arranging them in their physical settings.

4. A set of possible solutions: alternative grade organizations, patterns of school use, abandonment for outmoded and/or unsafe schools and needed new construction or closings (or both).

5. A choice among alternatives for a preferred course of action; a justification for the alternative selected; the preparation of the time sequence for the action to be taken; and a cost analysis of the implications of the selected plan as against alternative options.

The second step is perhaps the most critical element—gathering a factual base for proceeding toward a decision. William Keough and Katherine Eisenberger developed a "facilities usage criteria test" for assessing a school's potential for closing, which appeared in *Declining Enrollment: What To Do,* published by the American Assn. of School Administrators.

A task force—or citizens advisory committee or study group—is the most widely used and successful means for arriving at a set of alternatives from which the final decision is made. It brings together representatives of various community groups to study the facts, discuss their concerns and try to arrive at a consensus on several options that would solve the problems and be acceptable to the majority of those affected.

Those who serve on such panels learn how difficult a process it is. They have an opportunity to review all the data and gather information on their own. They serve as a link between the school board, administration and the community, verifying the need for a decision and the complexity of trying to weigh all interests and be fair to all concerned. If they are truly representative and not chosen to endorse preconceived conclusions, and if their work is used—as it should be—as a recommendation for the board's decision, the charge of unilateral action can be avoided. The task force can take a great deal of the heat off both the board and the district administration. It can provide a rational approach to a highly emotional problem.

Releasing Test Scores

One area that still strikes fear into the hearts of many superintendents and boards of education across the country is the release of standardized test results and other national and state tests. For the results of educational assessment programs provide a yardstick, a device not only to measure the success of a school or a school district, but also to compare that school or that district to another one not very far away. And the comparison can be difficult.

A handbook by NSPRA on releasing test scores says: "At the local school district level, the quality of assessment communication to parents, staff members, community leaders and other important publics has been generally subpar, or even non-existent."

The handbook continues:

"For the school district, and even the local school itself, assessment can often be a no-win situation. If scores are low, community reaction is predictable (What's wrong?). If they're high, the immediate question may be 'Why aren't they higher?' In other words, whatever the situation, it is very risky to release test scores without first preparing the staff and community."

Some educators have argued forcefully that assessment test scores are an insignificant measure of student achievement. This approach to assessment just doesn't work today. As far as the outside world is concerned, tests wouldn't be used if they didn't mean anything. So, on the premise that the scores are important to everybody, begin your dissemination efforts by analyzing your publics and understanding what the scores will mean to each of them.

Dissemination Begins at Home

The dissemination plan, like charity, should begin at home. Before alerting the media, make sure the staff—and that means all school employees—understands what the tests are and what the resulting scores mean. Reporters have been known to zero in immediately on a school whose scores were particularly high—or low. The principal or others who shrug off the interviewer with an "Oh, we're not worried about that Mickey Mouse program" will undercut whatever communication efforts are made by the central office (or the immediate district or state.)

However, the scores should not be given to staff members so early that results will be gossiped about and leaked out before they're ready for release by the superintendent and board of education to the media. The task is to develop a timeline that provides a logical dissemination sequence and gets the test data in the hands of staff as rapidly as possible. After all, the purpose of assessment is to provide information that will help teachers improve instruction. This basic fact alone should dictate placing teachers early in the dissemination timeline.

Following the staff briefings, each principal can begin individual reports to inform his or her school community. Then the central office can call a news conference and put the district newsletter to press. Ideally, it can all happen within one week. Utopia would be for each school to make its report to its community coincide with the districtwide release, because the **real credibility lies at the local school level.**

To the Staff

As soon as the scores are available, the central office should hold a detailed briefing for principals. This should include an explanation of the entire program and a thorough analysis of the results, complete with charts and tables. The principals become, in effect, the first line of PR, because they must go back to their schools to conduct detailed briefings on their own. So before they leave, they should be well-versed in the scores as well as the PR "line" the district wants to take.

Now, it's the principals' turn to take the explanations, the charts, and the peptalks back to their schools and conduct similar sessions for their staffs. And this doesn't mean just the faculty, either. The secretary who answers the phone and the custodian who chats with his neighbor in the barber shop are also part of the school family. They cannot be ignored.

They should not be expected, of course, to master all the educational implications of the scores, but they should have a general picture and understand the significance and purpose of assessment. Remember, to neighbors and casual acquaintances, they work for the school, and consequently their opinions carry a lot of authority in their social groups. The principal, therefore, should give the entire school staff a general briefing, outlining the major implications so that if any employee is confronted by a citizen in the supermarket, he or she will be able to respond confidently, "Yes, we've already made plans to beef up our reading instruction, but generally we were pretty pleased with the results." (Note that when they're involved in a program, it's "we." When they're left out, more often than not, it's "they.")

To the Parents

The teachers, however, need and should want a deeper understanding of the testing program and its ramifications to prepare them for the parents who want to know what all this means to their children. If the scores are below average, does this mean theirs is a "bad" school? How do their children's scores compare with the school's or the district's? Once again, the teacher can destroy the credibility of the entire program if he or she responds, "Oh, we don't pay any attention to that sort of thing" or "Test scores don't mean anything." To parents, test scores mean a lot. They represent concrete evidence. They "show" whether kids are learning or not learning. Downplaying their importance will only sound like an effort to evade responsibility, and it will backfire.

If the scores are low, everybody shouldn't sit around wringing their hands, but should think in terms of what can be done to bring them up. If they're high, the public relations problem is considerably lessened, but this should not be a cue to take bows. Staff response, rather, should be in terms of what they intend to do to keep them high.

To the Media

Once the schools and their staffs are informed, the next step should be to release the results to the media.

Like it or not, it is the media in most communities that transmit, and more importantly, interpret your test results to the public. Certainly, parents are concerned, on an individual basis, about the test scores for their own children, but it is the media which paint the big picture for the community. Thus, if you are going to get fair and objective treatment on test results, you must be prepared to work with the media. If you're not prepared, you're asking for trouble.

But why release test scores at all? Because, as is so painfully apparent in society today, anything you try to withhold, cover up, or hedge on in any way is viewed far more critically by the media and the public when it is eventually uncovered. If you don't release scores publicly now, the pressure will grow because so many other school systems across the country do release test results and people will eventually begin to ask, if they aren't already asking, "what have you got to hide?"

> So the key is to work with the news media as your key for full, frank, honest and objective dissemination of test results.

NSPRA's handbook on releasing test results offers some tips for the superintendent conducting the press conference at which the results are released: "The administrator who is schooled in the ways of media has a brief summary prepared and hands it out to the reporters, even before giving them the test reports. He or she does not read from the summary, but reviews it verbally.

A superintendent could say, "We are pleased with the results, but the report does point up some weaknesses, such as in fifth grade reading and seventh grade math. As soon as we received these test results we studied these areas. We plan to use specialists working in the elementary and junior high schools to get to the roots of these problems and work to solve them."

In 30 seconds, the superintendent has taken all the ammunition out of the reporters' guns and set the stage for a positive approach. The school system, it turns out, is taking all this in stride, has the situation well in hand, and is pleased to share it with the world.

Please note it was the superintendent who took charge of the news conference, not the public relations officer or testing director. The superintendent can and should defer to the experts when the questions are technical, but the superintendent is the spokesperson the media wants. If he or she is not there, and even if the other officials acquit themselves admirably, the media will still want comments from the superintendent.

To the Public

Now you have to brace for the impact of the news on your external publics.

At this stage the parents take their questions to the school staff. They may even ask their children, so a smart principal won't overlook that audience either.

Think how much a parent's mind would be eased if 12-year-old Jill would come home and say, "We got our test scores back today and our teacher said we did pretty well except in arithmetic so we worked on a lot of problems and I think I understand it better." Scratch one worried mother.

For the most part, however, the schools will feel the impact of parent concerns, while the central office will get it from the rest of the community and perhaps even from local government officials. And it won't take long to find out how well you did in your public relations planning. If you did a good job, expect things to be quiet. But if you didn't, the phone will ring off the hook.

Strikes

It is no secret that communication plays perhaps the single most vital role in the complexities and emotions of a school strike. Good communication can help prevent a strike; it can help bring order out of chaos during a strike, and it can be the adhesive that puts the broken pieces back together again after the strike is over.

J. William Jones, director of information services for the Philadelphia (Pa.) public schools and author of the NSPRA book, *School Labor Strife: Rebuilding the Team,* notes that "Clearly, today, the mood of the nation is changing in relation to strikes, both in the public and the private sector." There is little question that as public education courses somewhat roughly through the 1980s, negotiations is a two-edged sword," he says.

"One edge is economy. Not only are taxpayers up in arms about increased taxes on top of escalating costs of food, clothing, housing and transportation in the marketplace, but the 1980 census indicates that close to 72 percent of those taxpayers have no children attending public schools.

"Thus, school boards have two alternatives. One is drastically slashing budgets, and with them the alredy suspect quality of public education. The other is heaping increased taxes upon rebelling taxpayers, almost three-quarters of whom feel they receive no direct benefit from the public schools.

"The other edge is public confidence in public education. If school boards opt for slashed budgets and tough stances against union demands, a battle usually ensues. Them against us. Teachers against the administration and the board. Threats of strikes. Strikes. Emotion. Charge, countercharge. Sometimes violence.

"And the public is out there watching various factions of the school family take sides and do battle. 'Who needs public schools anyway?' 'The hell with 'em!' 'Let 'em fight!' 'This proves that they're not worth our support.'

"Thus, not only school districts but major corporations—faced with similar problems are, either through foresight or downright necessity, moving toward joint, cooperative, partner-oriented solutions not only to problems of wages and working conditions, but to problems of productivity and accountability."

Says *Newsweek Magazine:* "The changing economic environment is producing major changes in issues at the bargaining table." The magazine quotes David Lewin, a Columbia (N.Y.) University professor and labor analyst. Says Lewin: "Many companies have opened their books to unions and given them a broader role as a partner in the survival of the business."

"The dominance of criteria in bargaining," he says, "is changing rapidly from comparability and cost-of-living to ability to pay and productivity." Adds *Newsweek:* "At the plan level, more and more unions are cooperating with companies in problem solving committees and other mechanisms for improving product quality and productivity."

The situation is much the same in education. Two new systems are "Collective Gaining" in the Forest Park (Ill.) Public Schools and "Integrative Bargaining" in the Livermore (Calif.) Unified School District. Both are proven efforts to substitute cooperative conciliation-oriented, mutual-respect methods of problem solving for the standard we/them, win/lose, good/bad guy bargaining that threatens not only the public image, but also the very economic survival of so many school districts across the country.

Communicating Isn't Easy

Communicating sounds simple, and it should be. But anyone who has been caught in the middle of the whirlpool that is a school strike knows from sad experience that the simple act of communicating just isn't simple anymore.

Communicating effectively is seldom easy; it requires planning, effort, understanding and follow-through. Communicating effectively in the tense atmosphere which often surrounds a strike requires redoubled effort, greater understanding and increased attention to proper planning.

As one principal told a seminar session on school strikes at a recent convention, "You'd better be prepared. It can happen anywhere."

So, from the beginning of negotiations, plenty of intensive planning should be going into a procedure to communicate accurately, clearly and quickly with the media, staff, parents and community in case of an impasse.

For in all but those Utopian situations where management and union amicably reach a settlement, shake hands and live happily after, somewhere along the line the management negotiating team will inevitably have to take its case to the public.

It may come in answer to the union's public relations campaign; it may come by order of the board of education when a strike is inevitable; or it may come after pressure from the community to let them know where things stand. No matter the impetus, it will almost always come.

Taking Your Case to the Public

David Rossie, education editor for the Binghamton (N.Y.) *Evening Press*, told a crisis communication seminar sponsored by the New York State School Boards Association, "School boards that behave as if they have a lot to hide usually do."

The management negotiating team would do well to remember the advice of these two reporters as it plans to communicate its position to the public.

Dealing with the Media

Once the management team makes the decision to go to the public and the media, several points should be followed.

- □ **Don't tell them what to write.** A school management spokesperson telling a reporter what he or she should report is just about the same as a reporter telling an educator how to educate.
- □ **Present a statement** in writing for the record but don't hesitate to answer reporters' questions about it. No one can put everything in one statement and it is the reporter's job to ask questions to clarify every issue.
- □ **Don't attempt to speak "off the record"** unless asked to by the media. If a media person requests a background, off-the-record conference on a negotiations issue or issues, that's one thing. Oblige them. But don't stand up in front of media representatives, issue a statement and then tell them it's off the record. In this case, if they don't agree first to consider a statement or portion of it off the record, they have absolutely no obligation not to report what you say.

☐ **Don't use jargon.** You're not bargaining over multivariate cognitive and affective educational objectives. You're bargaining over a variety of educational programs. You're not hung up over the number of language arts supportive personnel. They're reading aides. Keep it simple and clear; short words, short sentences and short paragraphs.

☐ **Be scrupulously accurate.** Off-hand, unresearched, inaccurate remarks to the media will quickly come back over the bargaining table to haunt the negotiating team.

☐ **Don't call the other side names.** Regardless of the old "sticks and stones may break my bones" advice, names can hurt you, if you use them.

☐ **Don't play favorites.** Many school boards and superintendents have a favorite reporter. And that's fine if it helps in getting day-to-day school news in the paper or on the air during the regular school term. But if you start playing favorites during the clamor of news coverage of a major strike, the rest of the media will seek other sources—like the union leaders, for instance.

☐ **Don't ever say, "This is our final offer."** In bargaining there rarely is such a thing as a "final" offer. You know it, the media knows it, and the teachers and staff know it. More credibility is lost by boards of education through "final" offers than through just about any other bargaining ploy.

☐ **Don't try to obtain publicity by pressure.** If a newspaper or radio or TV station is independent and objective—and most are—NO ONE, outside of its own corporate management, and in some cases not even them, tells a news outlet what news to print or to broadcast.

☐ **Above all, be honest, accurate, frank and friendly.**

Parents and the Community

While the news media, in most cases, will be the quickest way to reach parents and the community during negotiations, it can not and must not be considered the only way.

For one thing, the media, by its nature, can use just a capsule of your negotiations position in its daily or weekly reports. Some specific points you might consider crucially important to parents and the community might be considered by the media not as newsworthy as some of the more immediate financial or political aspects of the negotiations process. Thus it may never see print or be presented on the air.

The answer, then, for parents and community, is a series of **fact sheets** presenting management's step-by-step view of the negotiation's process.

These fact sheets should be just that—**FACT Sheets**—not propaganda leaflets geared to pull the wool over the collective eyes of the community.

Experience has shown that parents and community want the following kinds of information:

- What are the issues, and what is their financial impact on the pocketbook of the parent/taxpayer?
- What about the union's charge that by opposing their requests you're diminishing the quality of education offered to youngsters in the school district? If the board has its way in negotiations, how would the contract affect the quality of education?
- If there is a strike, will the schools be open? Will there be transportation and lunches? Will the children be safe? Might school buildings be closed at midday during a strike, sending children of working parents out on the street with no adult supervision?
- Whom or where can a parent call to get up-to-the-minute information about the possibility of a strike?
- Can parents help out in the schools if there is a strike?

The key with parents and the community, as with the newsmedia, is to stick to the facts on the issues at hand. Leave out opinions about the employee organizations, however tempted you may be to editorialize about their behavior, their personal attacks, or any other diversion planned to take the spotlight off issues like salaries, class size, length of the school day, extracurricular pay, preparation time and health and welfare benefits.

All right, but how do you get this information to parents?

It's a good question, and the first answer is how not to do it. And the one process that should be avoided is sending letters home with students. In essence, you're using the students against their teachers and the repercussions will be considerable.

It's like waving a red flag in the teacher association's face, inviting open resistance on the part of the classroom teacher and a confrontation you don't need any part of, particularly during what more than likely is a delicate time in the negotiations process.

The answer is the mails. Small school districts should have a list of every household with children in the schools. A full set of mailing labels can be prepared ahead of time.

Larger school districts must have lists of all key communicators in the community: PTA officers, civic and community groups, block associations, community service groups, business leaders, bankers, beauticians—just about anyone with an interest in the community and its schools.

When negotiations are at an impasse; when the teachers' association has gone public; whenever the board of education decides to take its case to the community: all these contacts must be fully informed by fact sheets that are, in fact, factual.

Communicating With the Staff

When a strike is imminent, perhaps your most important communication must go to staff: to the staff directly affected by the strike as well as to the rest of the school district employees. They, above all, must know, concisely and clearly, the administration's position on the issues in contention.

Such a communiqué is imperative not only to clarify the administration's position on the issues, but to dispel whatever misinformation has been circulated about the conflict between the union and management. It is important, in the long run, that every school district employee be fully and accurately informed of the positions separating management and the union.

The following guidelines, taken from the book, *School Labor Strife: Rebuilding The Team,* should be followed:

☐ Content should be absolutely factual, low-key and non-threatening.

☐ Don't editorialize. If the strike is illegal in your area, say so. Cite the state law, chapter and verse.

☐ Explain why you have rejected certain union demands that now form the principal strike issues.

☐ Don't tar all teachers with the same brush if you are having problems with the association and its leaders. Differentiate between the negotiators and the rest of the employees.

☐ List concessions management has already made.

☐ Detail your "last" offer to the teachers' association. Explain why, particularly financially, you feel you shouldn't go any further.

☐ Send the communiqué to every staff member—not just the group threatening to strike, but all employee groups—professional and support staff members.

☐ Remember that there is a fine line between being argumentative and setting the record straight. Stay on the straight side even if it pains you to do so. The reader's reaction will depend largely on the tone of the communication.

The Communication Center

When school employees strike, the impact on the community is determined by public opinion. Strike communication, how it is handled and when it occurs, will determine whether public opinion supports the school board/district or the strikers.

A communication center where strike and negotiations information can be gathered, analyzed and communicated in a systematic, professional and dispassionate way to the many publics affected by a strike is the keystone of any communication plan.

It is in the communication center that the critical management decisions—except those requiring board action—will be made during a strike. Perhaps the most important aspect of the communication center and the information developed there is the establishment of credibility. There has to be credibility behind pupil attendance figures and the reports on the number of teachers reporting for work. A network and reporting plan must be established and maintained between the center and each school building plan.

Each day the communications center will need to report on:

- How many teachers were in their classrooms
- How many teachers were out of their classrooms
- How many students were in school
- How many replacement teachers were in the classrooms
- How many support staff and parent volunteers were there
- What kinds of questions and concerns are being telephoned in to each school
- Any incidents of vandalism or violence
- How many schools are open
- If there are regular schedules
- If buses are running
- If lunches are being served
- If it is safe to send children to school
- If teaching and learning are really happening
- If students will be penalized if they stay home
- What the district is doing to bring the situation to an end.

After the Strike

The only thing all strikes have in common is that one day they end. And then begins perhaps the most critical task of all: putting it all back together again.

Anne Barkelew, vice president for corporate public relations with Dayton Hudson Corp. in Minneapolis, Minn., (formerly PR director of the Los Angeles County [Calif.] Schools) proposes 12 basic rules school systems should follow for recovery after a strike, with a warning that "they're easy to give, but sometimes very difficult to implement."

1. Forget the past. It's water under the dam. Concentrate on the present and the future. Don't rehash. Rule out classroom discussion of the strike. Likewise, avoid strike discussions in faculty meetings. Concentrate on instructional strategies for making up lost time.

2. Forget post-strike social events and get-togethers for a while. Experience shows that most of the time they'll only rekindle strike animosities.

3. A spirit of reconciliation must be adopted and promulgated by the board, the superintendent and the entire administrative team. Anything that discriminates has to be rooted out and destroyed.

4. Schedule principal workshops on interpersonal relations. Consider hiring a psychologist to conduct the workshop.

5. Maintain, at all costs, a positive attitude. Be friendly, warm and sincere and be contagious with it.

6. Disseminate the terms of the settlement widely, with briefings for the management team, instantly, if not sooner. The minute you get a settlement, call your administrators in. If it's at night, call them in at 7 a.m. If it's during the day, call them in immediately. Brief them thoroughly on the terms of the settlement.

7. Help teachers put their best foot forward. After a strike, Barkelew says, "the image of teachers must be one of being helpful, concerned, professional and dedicated to education."

8. Stack the board meeting agenda to make it "pro-instruction." Emphasize instruction. Talk about curriculum. Feature successful educational programs.

9. Educate everyone about school finance. "The basic issues at stake in any strike," Barkelew contends, "are money and power."

10. Start a new project. Form a citizens committee. Start a new curriculum study.

11. After a strike, "be very, very consistent in your behavior. It is not the time to set new rules, to issue new, sweeping directives from on high, to crack down on something you've let go for years."

12. Emphasize the importance of the school district school staff. Not only the superintendent, but cabinet level administrators also should visit schools and classrooms, "being visible and visibly interested in staff, all staff."

Desegregation

School administrators, teachers, parents and community leaders met in Denver, Colo., in the mid-70's for three days to discuss successes in desegregation efforts across the country, to identify common ingredients, and to put together blueprints for communities where desegregation has an unfinished agenda.

It became evident at that meeting that despite the headlines and the battles and the burning of buses in some communities, desegregation had come amid relative peace and calm in others. Once again, as is the trend throughout this book, planning, communication and community involvement were keys to the kingdom of success.

The conference was sponsored by the then U.S. Office of Education and the Council of Chief State School Officers in cooperation with the American Assn. of School Administrators, The Council of the Great City Schools, the National Assn. of State Boards of Education and the Education Commission of the States. It was coordinated by NSPRA and it came up with the following recommendations for dealing constructively with the problems of desegregation:

Ways To Develop Positive Attitudes

☐ The school board, superintendent and top administrative team must set the tone. They must make a firm commitment to parental and community involvement, rather than giving it only "lip service." Parents and the community must not be used to "rubber stamp" decisions that have been made at the top.

☐ Establish quick, clear, concise communication channels. School districts must mount a massive communication effort, either through their own communication personnel or through consultation with a professional public relations firm. In addition to handling the media, there must be communication with key community groups and business establishments, from banks and large corporations to gas stations, beauty parlors and neighborhood grocery stores. There must be a rumor-control center where a parent or other member of the community can get either an immediate answer or a quick return call on any question, problem or concern. Such a center should operate 24 hours a day, with recordings during non-working hours.

☐ Both district wide and school task forces must be formed and informed—and must be representative of the community. They should be given specific responsibilities and a timetable and should be dealt with openhandedly and objectively.

☐ Assure both parents and the community that the quality of education will not be compromised by desegregation and that desegregated pupils will be safe in their schools. Sometimes a symbolic effort can be very significant, such as the school superintendent riding or driving buses during the first few days of desegregation.

☐ Work with and strengthen existing organizations, rather than "reinventing the wheel." Enlist the help of PTAs, church groups, ethnic organizations and community and civic associations.

☐ Consider using consultants skilled in community analysis to recommend the best ways to offer human relations training for existing community groups.

☐ Those responsible for schools must anticipate and develop a plan before one is mandated.

Working With The Staff

☐ Mandate and fund inservice training in human relations for all staff—professional and non-professional. However, again, the best influence on staff is by example. The school district leadership should firmly develop behavioral goals and objectives with the staff, and central office administration should be highly visible in the schools during the desegregation process.

☐ School district policies should require that staffs be desegregated, preferably before student desegregation.

☐ The school administration must anticipate the problems that will be faced by the staff in dealing with desegregation and should have ready suggested solutions and materials that will be helpful. The central administration should have a human relations staff to coordinate inservice training and to help on individual problems.

☐ The staff must be involved in selecting and developing multiethnic, multiracial texts and curricula dealing with equality and human relations.

☐ Before desegregation, work with teacher training institutions to provide special training for those who want to teach in a desegregated environment. Practice teaching should be in integrated schools, rather than an "antiseptic" laboratory class.

☐ Involve the leadership of the teachers' organizations in plans for staff desegregation and inservice training.

Working With Students

☐ School district policies must assure that students will be given a major role in helping to carry out desegregation. This involvement must be both in the development of plans and in their implementation.

☐ Form integrated teams of students to work on problems in desegregating schools. The teams might visit other schools in successfully desegregated school systems to get ideas. They also should be used to help orient students in feeder schools.

☐ Provide human relations training programs for students with constant follow-up and evaluation to prevent problems from festering.

☐ School district policies must assure that discipline procedures are fair and equitable to all students and that students are free from intimidation and fear.

☐ School districts must develop multiracial, multiethnic curricula relating to the achievements of all minority groups to help improve students' attitudes about each other.

☐ Extracurricular student activities should be carried out with no loss of leadership status. Students should be encouraged to establish structures to assure equal representation on teams, as cheerleaders,

Small School Districts

Small school districts need PR, too.

And with the proper commitment, it can be done on a limited budget. And it definitely brings results.

Small rural school districts can accomplish a lot of school public relations work in two to four hours a week with cash outlay of less than $1,000 a year, according to an "old hand" in that kind of district.

Norman Maguire, executive director, Minnesota Association of School Administrators, says he's never been in a district large enough to have a hired PR person—full-time or part-time. "But school community relations is just as important in a small district as in a large one—maybe more so. And you don't have to spend a lot to do a lot."

Maguire's experience in Minnesota schools leads him to think of "small" as 200 to 700 enrollment, K-12. The former superintendent of Great Falls, Minn., believes that an administrator, a teacher or a lay person may be designated to coordinate public relations, but if no one else is available it may need to be a personal responsibility of the superintendent. "I contend you have to do it," he says. "People want us to be accountable."

Maguire says you should start by developing policies. The board of education has to say it wants public relations and will support it financially. For less than $1,000 a year, the board can print necessary materials, he says. Once a system is operating, it will yield good results from two to four hours of work a week, plus clerical time to do typing and mailing. Maguire aims efforts at three publications staff, student council, and other leadership roles. For example, student council presidents from schools that are being integrated could serve as co-presidents.

☐ Activity buses to allow students to remain after school must be provided by the school district.

Busing

☐ Avoid buzz words such as "forced busing." Call it "pupil reassignment" or "transportation policies."

audiences—staff, parents and other district residents and those outside the district who are prospective residents or staff.

An essential item, he says, is a report of school board meetings for the staff, available the next morning or no later than noon. "Remember the high credibility of classified staff in the community," he points out. "They need to have facts, immediately, to relay to their families and friends."

Further, no one person can handle school-community relations for the district—it involves the entire school community of students, faculty, administrators, other staff and school board. "Spend a few minutes in a workshop before school begins on the importance of community relations," he urges. "Teachers are not in the school just to teach. They need visibility and involvement in the com-

munity. This will do much for the 'image' of school people and take away the 'transient' aspect."

Maguire says the small school district must set up an ongoing program with a regular flow of information, rather than a crisis-to-crisis approach. "Be willing to try anything that looks beneficial to education in your district. Nobody wins ballgames without leading off first base. Constantly evaluate what you are doing—seek feedback from the consumers. If it doesn't work, quit it."

Work closely with the news media which serve the district—find out what they want and when—and cooperate, he said. But don't rely entirely on news media. Put together a newsletter for staff, parents and the community, and make sure that anything from the school is well written.

☐ Try to make the busing plan two-way, treating all segments of the student population equitably.

☐ Emphasize the program advantages of reassigning students—quality education at the end of the ride.

☐ Make sure that the specifics of the busing program are well known. Arrange for parents and children to ride the buses together on the assigned route before desegregation begins. Hold open houses at the new schools at the end of the bus ride.

☐ Emphasize safety precautions—and let the community know that this is a strong policy. Train bus drivers to handle discipline problems, but also establish training and behavior codes for students. Let parents know what the standards are. Use bus stop monitors, if necessary, for safety and to help students develop self-discipline for the bus ride.

☐ Hold open hearings on bus routes so that parents can have some involvement in the busing plan.

☐ Set reasonable time limits on the length of bus rides and try to keep drivers on the same route.

Media Relationships

☐ Involve the media in desegregation plans. Meet regularly with editors and management and give them roles in developing the plan. Ask their cooperation in developing informational public service programming that will put desegregation in a proper perspective.

☐ Plan a media campaign that will balance the attention given to desegregation. Prepare information for the media on numerous other educational programs in the school system—to convey the theme that education of all children is still the purpose of the schools.

☐ Explore the use of all types of media coverage—e.g., community newspapers, cable TV systems. Representative student contributions to local newspapers and TV programs can give a community an expanded perspective of what is happening inside schools. Communications should be multilingual, where necessary.

CHAPTER THIRTEEN

Building-Level Public Relations

There is little question that good school public relations begins at the top, with a strong commitment from the superintendent and a comprehensive policy from the board of education.

But there is no question that the most effective component of a school district's public relations program is at the **school-building level.**

It is at the local school building that the parents are either turned on or turned off; that the community is either welcomed or ignored; and where the child is either motivated to learn or allowed to wither on the educational vine.

In the long run, the "good news" about education is best told to the parents and taxpayers by the students themselves. Happy, enthusiastic, challenged, learning children are the best possible public relations program any school system can have.

And perhaps next best is a school that goes out of its way to communicate with its community; that builds communication with the public into its daily routine; that makes a concerted effort to reach out and encourage two-way understanding with its publics.

The process involves both bringing parents and key community communicators into the school and reaching out to those who don't make it in. The following are some field-tested ideas on both:

Bringing Them In

☐ **Have an open-door visitation policy.** Invite parents and community members to school and repeat the invitation often—in newsletters, in the parents' handbook, in report card stuffers, by special, personal invitations.

☐ **Have a visitors' day** for prospective students and their parents—not just for the entering class but for those at any level who may be considering attendance at your school. Publicize it well throughout the community/neighborhood.

- ☐ **Hold a principal's coffee at the school** on a regular basis to draw parents and other visitors to the school for informal discussions.
- ☐ **Publish a schedule for telephone conferences with teachers,** specialists and administrators. Set a vareity of times.
- ☐ **Seek and encourage** visits and participation by nonparents.
- ☐ **Hold tours** for businesspersons; have a grandparents day; invite people in the neighborhood to drop in frequently.

Reaching Out

- ☐ Encourage "good news" calls from teachers. Although these require willing participation on the part of your staff to be successful, you can provide basic guidelines for calls and ensure that privacy and a telephone are available at convenient times during the school day so that teachers will be more likely to act on the suggestion.
- ☐ Encourage elementary teachers to summarize the events and classroom progress of the day with their students and urge them to "tell your parents what you learned at school today."
- ☐ Just as you may have block parents for safety, have neighborhood volunteers to provide a channel for two-way communication: ask someone in each neighborhood to contact you with community concerns, explain new programs, to get the word out and back to the school.
- ☐ Hold small, informal neighborhood meetings in the homes of volunteers led by parents or students your staff has trained to explain special programs, discuss curriculum changes and answer questions. These are particularly helpful for parents of the entering class or newcomers to the area.
- ☐ Organize a speakers bureau of students and teachers for parent and community group meetings.
- ☐ Take classes into the community: band rehearsals or art classes at shopping centers, for example, give the public a first-hand look at how a program works.
- ☐ Videotape learning sessions such as math and reading classes, civics, Latin, debate, etc., and show these to civic groups and service clubs. These schools in action programs are worth a thousand words.

A PR Plan for the Local School

Whether an elementary school, middle, junior high, senior high, vocational-technical, magnet, or alternative school—you already have a public relations plan. The question is whether it is planned or it just happened.

If you aren't sure, start now to find out. Hold a School Communications Workshop for your entire staff—professional and support. Involve them in developing a PR plan for the school year—one that recognizes the critical importance of communicating with **all your publics—internal and external.** Be sure that the plan covers the following 11 points:

1. **Staff communication and involvement.** A school's own staff is the key to good public relations.
2. **Parent communication.** Many traditional ways of communicating with parents are not working as well as they once did. Try these suggestions:
   - Parent workshops—not only after school, but before school, in the evening and on Saturdays.
   - Homework hotlines—where parents can call at certain hours in the evening to get assistance over the telephone from teachers on homework problems or other questions.
3. **Principal communication.** Use every opportunity possible to speak to parents and to visit groups explaining the school program and the principal's role in it. Be close to your staff, visible in the halls, take over a class now and then. Take an active role in the community.
4. **Publications.** Carefully plan your efforts to communicate with pictures and the printed word to tell the school story through publications such as: a school handbook, newsletter, program and curriculum guide(s), annual report, a school calendar, informational brochure, etc.
5. **Regular school visitation program.** Invite parents and non-parents to the school to "see for themselves" and repeat the invitation often.
6. **A policy of reaching out to the community.** Encourage volunteers—including senior citizens—to help students learn.
7. **Establish a Speakers Bureau.** This can be composed of your school staff and students. Develop a speech kit with slides or videotape about your school. Design a handout telling success stories of present and past students to be distributed.
8. **Set up a system of key communicators.** Identify those persons who know what's going on in the community and put them to work on your team. They can be effective not only in times of crisis and rumor, but in calmer times, too, when good news is unobstructed by emotional charge and countercharge.
9. **A Citizens Advisory Committee.** Invite a group of parents, non-parents, neighborhood business leaders, staff and students to serve on a special public relations committee to provide you with input about communication needs.

10. **Student communication.** Principals with good internal communication programs agree just about unanimously that students are key communicators. Build in special listening opportunities, be visible and valuable. Hold rap sessions with students, invite small groups to a "brown bag" lunch, hold press conferences for student newspaper editors and establish recognition programs.

11. **Help parents help their children learn.** Provide sessions and materials:

    • Provide special opportunities for single parents to develop support groups.

    • Provide extended day programs for children of working parents.

    • Be aware of special needs of children of divorced parents: offer conferences for both parents and report cards for each if requested. Provide special programs to help these children.

Go Internal First

In meeting the critical needs for external communication at the building level, too many principals either overlook the need for internal communication or take it for granted. This can be a fatal mistake.

If staff, students and parents don't promote the school, all the key communicators and community advisory boards in the world won't overcome a poor school image generated from within the school family.

Are You Listening?

One of the most important tools of the principal is feedback. But feedback is only as good as you, the principal want to make it. What's happening out there? Do you know? Try these ideas from NSPRA's "Principals' Survival Packet":

☐ **Staff listening sessions.** Get out—go around. Learn what staff members are thinking. Visit with them on their time and on their turf— during lunch breaks, inservice, etc. Show them you care and are interested and appreciative. Don't defend. Listen and show your appreciation. Inform where possible, and pass along concerns and suggestions to proper persons.

☐ **Parent-teacher phone calls.** Divide up the parents in your schools among all the teachers. During the year, see that every parent gets at least one "good news call." Then, ask parents what they think about your school and what kinds of information they want. Have sheets prepared on which the teachers can write down responses.

☐ **Question cards.** Place cards titled "I HAVE A QUESTION" around the school building and key locations around the school neighbor-

The Staff

Following are suggestions for a principal interested in generating better communication with his or her staff:

☐ Meetings should have a specific purpose, a structured agenda, and a topic of interest to all. Don't dominate. Two-way communication works best.

☐ Post staff announcements on well-located bulletin board, in the faculty lounge, and put in mailboxes. Always post copies of materials sent home to parents.

☐ Publish a weekly staff newsletter that reflects a variety of interests and concerns. Mention hobbies, achievements and community activities, as well as strictly school-related items.

☐ Write little notes with positive personal messages that say you see your staff as people.

☐ Increase your approachability. Encourage input at a specific time during the day when many of your staff are free.

☐ Vary your lunch periods to socialize with a larger number of your staff in a casual atmosphere.

☐ Encourage professional growth. Commend your staff when they have done a good job. And remember to say, "thank you," preferably in writing.

☐ Be receptive to new ideas and be willing to facilitate constructive change.

hood—such as shopping centers, banks, etc. Show the staff and community that school leaders really want to listen. And, respond within 24 hours!

☐ **"I have an idea" card.** Ask for ideas that will improve the school. Place these cards in the same locations as the question card and promise people that they will hear from you within seven days after you receive a card.

☐ **Mini polls.** Take an idea from the pros and have a little short quiz developed for teacher conferences, school programs, meetings, etc. On a card ask if the meeting was successful. How could it have been improved? Seek suggestions for ways the school could serve better. Remember to ask if another time would have been better—if so, what time, date and place? This is important as districts gear programs to meet needs of two-career parents, single parents, etc.

☐ **Coffees.** Take the school program to the neighborhood. Ask for volunteers to host small neighborhood meetings in their homes.

Teachers—A Vital Link

Teachers need PR training, too. That's the consensus of most school public relations professionals who recognize that, next to the students themselves, the teacher is the most influential PR person for parents at the building level.

Here are some good public relations techniques that your teachers can use, taken from the pages of *It Starts in the Classroom,* a communication newsletter for classroom teachers and administrators published by NSPRA.

- □ Teachers should be alert to innovative projects, student achievements and interesting crafts that would be newsworthy for local papers, TV and/or radio.
- □ Home visits—an essential to reach working parents/minority parents if they are unable to come to school functions.

PR Tips for Teachers

□ Speak Up for Education! Wherever you go, show your pride in your profession and share exciting education news from your classroom and school district. Be a PR ambassador for your schools.

□ Be alert to special classroom projects that warrant media coverage. Contact the media directly or alert your building principal and/or district information officer. Remember that you need to make all contacts two weeks to 10 days in advance of the event. Don't overlook the opportunity of a feature story which does not have a time element.

□ Correct papers with comments and correction marks that will be understandable to both students and parents.

□ Extend yourself to students who need extra help with a flexible schedule for after-school or before-school meetings. This is particularly important on the secondary school level with students who are involved in extra-curricular activities.

□ Flexibility of schedules should also be available for parent meetings to conform to their work hours. Many schools are holding parent teacher conferences in neighborhood areas, during evening hours, and on the weekends.

□ Start a monthly class newsletter for reports to parents, or send home Friday folders with student work and a reply form for parents to complete show-

□ Happygrams or congratulatory notes—to parents whenever Charlie or Betty does an exceptionally good job in classroom or at a special event.
□ Children love to be called by their nicknames. Teachers should find out immediately during the first week of school what their students prefer to be called.
□ Many teachers have special skills and expertise that can be shared with their students.

Publications

One important area of school public relations too often overlooked by school building staffs is the area of publications.

ing they read the material and provide space for them to ask any questions they have. (Reply by phone or note as quickly as possible.)
□ Hold a "lunch with parents day." This can be with the students and parents or with parents and teacher only.
□ At parent-teacher conferences: be prepared with a written list of strengths and weaknesses to discuss, specifically those weaknesses that need to be corrected; have any test reports written out so that parents can take results home and not have to absorb facts and figures reported verbally; have samples of student's work available—the best examples and those demonstrating areas needing improvement; include any specialists working with student in the conference or have a report from the specialists. (On the secondary level many teachers are including students in the conference.)
□ Utilize non-parent as well as parent resource people in the classroom to enrich classes and "involve community." Seek to involve senior citizens for an intergenerational activity with the students.
□ Keep parents informed about anything new or different in the classroom—projects with extra homework, long-term assignments requiring special work, new techniques, etc. Explain to parents so they will understand and support your efforts.

Says Kenneth L. Weir, director of school-community relations for the North Penn School District, Lansdale, Pa.: "Every basic school communication program should include a carefully planned effort using words and pictures to tell the school story.

What Can the Principal Do about Publications?

Weir has some suggestions for building-level publications:
1. The school principal must understand the importance of publications.

The Student Handbook

In putting together a handbook of school policies, procedures and information for students and parents, the following information is generally what parents and students want to know:

School Policies
- Attendance
- Grading and report cards
- Conferences
- Discipline
- Emergency school closings
- Homework
- Trips
- Eligibility for participation in athletics
- Access to student records

School Calendar
- Holidays
- Inservice days; schools open but not for students
- PTA meetings
- Annual events: concerts, science fairs, commencement, etc.
- Athletic events
- Report card days and end of grading periods
- Dates of open house, conferences, etc.

Staff Information
- Key contact people: administrators, counselors, department chairpersons
- Specialists

General Information
- School hours
- School meals
- Fees
- Extracurricular programs
- Volunteer programs
- Parent-teacher organizations
- Student insurance
- Emergency care procedures
- Transportation for handicapped children

Curriculum Information
- Meaning of "competency-based curriculum"; what changes it will make in your school program
- Team teaching, multi-age grouping, and other variations from traditional structures, where applicable
- Required and elective programs

2. Invite a small student/faculty/parent committee to join in a review of the publications of the past year.
3. Invite a community advisory committee to meet monthly, quarterly, or as needed for review of school publications problems. Include newspaper reporter, PR-type employees from local industry, and parents with related education or experience.
4. Rank publications according to priority. Improve only one at a time—one each year if that is all that is feasible. (Don't try to do it all at once.)
5. Advocate that appropriate teachers be given extra-duty contracts to write about, edit, or photograph the school story. Make a visible commitment to improve publications.
6. Identify student writers and photographers who can be given released time to work on school publications.
7. Arrange with parent or senior citizen volunteers for writing, editing and photography.
8. Use student newspaper and yearbook staff as much as possible.
9. Arrange with local newspaper photographers to obtain extra prints for use in your school publications.
10. Develop comprehensive photo file in main office.
11. Build idea file of good publications from other schools.

Releasing Test Scores

To many school principals, communicating when things are going well is not much of a problem. It's always reasonable easy and enjoyable to spread good news.

But when problems arise, more often than not it's a different story. Few principals are equipped by training to handle crisis communication.

And the public disclosure of basic skills achievement or assessment test scores is most definitely a crisis to most building principals. Yet, with proper planning and procedures, it need not be.

As the first line of public information and relations at the individual school level, the principal has to be ready—and willing—to take an active role. Individual schools with unusually high—or low—scores may find themselves bombarded by reporters, but the majority of the buildings will be generally uncovered except for a cryptic column of numbers in a statistical summary. The parents of the children who attend those schools, however, are concerned and it's up to each principal to answer their questions in a satisfactory way.

A school-based information program is a must. It should be aimed at parents—those who read the districtwide or building results in the papers and wonder what they mean and those who don't read the papers at all. The latter group is larger than is generally acknowledged, and it is the most susceptible to back-fence gossip. In either case, the test result information is best received when it comes voluntarily from the school, not in response to an angry protest.

Here, culled from publications that communicate test results effectively, are some thoughts to consider when the time comes to tell the story of your school's testing program—whether at a large meeting, or in a parent-teacher conference.

- ☐ Avoid testing jargon. Use everyday words and keep your report as general as you can. What people want to know is what the results mean. Are the kids in the upper 25 percent or the lower 10 percent? Are they doing better this year than last?
- ☐ Don't downplay the importance of testing in the educational program. It's well and good to speak of the subjective elements of a good education—those factors that cannot be measured by a test, but such talk will never persuade a parent that a low score means you are still providing quality education.
- ☐ Statistics are for statisticians. A table or graph is necessary for those few readers who appreciate those things, but the average citizen will appreciate a narrative stressing concepts and avoiding all but the most critical figures.
- ☐ Accompany your report with details of what you intend to do about the results—especially the poor ones. Don't wait for a public outcry before explaining how you are beefing up your reading or math program. After all, isn't that what tests are for—to show you where you must put your emphasis?
- ☐ Face-to-face explanations are far more effective than cold newsletter articles. If the principal and teachers take time to explain the testing program, the results, and their implications for instruction at a parents' meeting, chances for understanding are greatly enhanced. All teachers should be formally and thoroughly briefed about the program so they can answer questions confidently—and not defensively—at parent conferences.
- ☐ Be frank and honest, but don't overlook any opportunity to brag. Because of the recent emphasis on the basics in most districts, chances are many of the scores are up. Never mind whether the statisticians are willing to call these increases "significant." People want to know you're moving in the right direction.

An assessment program is, in fact, an ideal vehicle for establishing an accountability dialogue with the community. Educators may argue that single listing of test results doesn't really tell much about an educational program, but they will have a difficult time convincing the community. So why not take advantage of the requirement to issue a report by incorporating it into a broader information package that tells where you've been, where you are, and where you hope to go?

Ideally, this should evolve into an annual effort because any reporting on school objectives should center on the year's progress toward attaining them. It sounds like a big project, and it is. But since it will require the involvement of the entire faculty in setting the objectives for the school, it will pay off instructionally as well as in good public relations.

An Annual Report

In the mid-70's the Montgomery County (Md.) Board of Education felt so strongly about the need to report assessment scores on a school-by-school basis that it mandated that each of the district's more than 200 schools issue an annual school progress report each year.

And the board issued detailed guidelines as to what the report should involve. These guidelines can provide a strong basis for giving any community an annual look at the accomplishments, structure and goals of their school:

1. **Community**—a description of the characteristics of the attendance area of the school, and a statement of the major community concerns as expressed by the PTA, advisory groups, letters and phone calls and surveys.
2. **Enrollment**—pertinent statistics showing trends and characteristics of the student body. Here is where the results of the standardized tests are reported, including an emphasis on those areas where the school scored a certain amount above, or below, the norm. This section can also include information on tests administered by the school, performance on college admissions tests, results of any follow-up study that may have been done on graduates, and so forth.
3. **Staff**—the number of full-time staff, both professional and support, their years of experience and level of training, and their assignments in the type of organizational plan used by the school.
4. **Building**—a description of the school plant itself—the capacity, number of rooms, special facilities, etc., with a description of how the building design affects the organization or program. Immediate plans for renovations or additions should be reviewed.
5. **Objectives**—for the past year, a list of the objectives and a discussion of how well the school did in attaining them; for the current year, a description of each objective, the strategy for attaining it and the evidence that will indicate success. The guidelines caution building principals that the setting of objectives requires the involvement of staff and community, and that each school objective

should be related to the information in the previous sections of the report.

Today, an increasing number of states have passed laws mandating annual reports by school districts and building by building. The alert principal, aware that in a good part, his or her success depends on the support and understanding of the school's programs by both parents and the community, welcomes this direction as a unique and valuable way to communicate. These reports when developed with the aid of parents, students, staff and community volunteers, can provide a balanced and realistic picture of progress within the building.

Bonnie Ellison, a past president of NSPRA and information director of the Northside (Texas) Independent School District, points out that there are other legal obligations requiring schools to communicate with the community. "When school disputes land in the courthouse, the judge invariably wants proof that the issues have been widely discussed and the decisions clearly communicated," Ellison says. "Always be prepared with proof."

Discipline

Another major communication problem that can be attacked effectively by the building principal and turned into a PR plus is **discipline.**

Here are some rules for parents in the area of discipline developed by the Fitzgerald Public Schools in Warren, Mich.:

1. **Rules:** Set rules and explain them. Don't use rules unless you plan to be consistent in enforcing them.
2. **Approval:** Give attention to good behavior. A little praise goes a long way. Remember, it is important to children what you think of them. How children conduct themselves depends on what they think of themselves.
3. **Ignoring:** Try not to give too much attention to bad behavior, unless it is serious. Some children continue to misbehave because they enjoy the attention they receive from parents who are constantly correcting them.
4. **Discipline:** If rules have been explained thoroughly, there is no need to continue to lecture and warn. Punishment for misbehavior that is considered serious does not have to be severe, but it should be quick, reasonable and related to the misbehavior. Tell your child it is his or her behavior that you disapprove of, not him or her.

5. **Participation:** Children need to learn to interact with adults. The gap between parents and children widens when they spend little time with each other. All kinds of activities and projects that are fun can be developed to help establish harmony. When children and parents are having fun together, the children respond positively and few serious discipline problems arise.

And Then, There's the Media

Then, perhaps, there is the biggest problem of all to many principals: communicating with the media.

It wasn't too long ago that reporters were a rarity at the local school building, except maybe during American Education Week. But today, many school districts with a strong public relations program encourage reporters to go out into the schools, where the good news lies, ready to be uncovered and reported.

But that's another worry for the harried principal without any training on how to deal with the media. Thus, unfortunately, the meeting of the reporter and the principal can be a communication disaster unless the principal is prepared, proud of his or her school, and willing to proclaim its merits frankly and objectively.

Good publicity depends on an awareness of what makes news in the first place and on continuing efforts to get the information about it to the right channels. Negative news gets coverage—for sure! But it takes conscious planning to get the good news out or to turn the media contact that begins unfavorably into a positive one for your school.

When They Contact You

Be accurate, be clear and be honest in all your dealings with reporters. A reluctance to answer questions that put the school in a bad light may be construed as concealment. Resist the urge to gloss over unpleasantness; deal forthrightly with issues. Fielding difficult questions and making complicated information comprehensible is easier if you are prepared. Here are some hints:

☐ Anticipate the information needed. Prepare a fact sheet.

☐ Anticipate especially the negative points likely to be raised and have a response ready.

☐ Make lemonade of the lemons by confronting issues directly. Acknowledge the problem; outline a course of action to correct it; invite questions. You can earn a fair hearing and an unbiased presentation by your willingness to be open with the news media.

When You Contact Them

You are the best judge of what is appropriate or important to publicize about your school. You will want to strike a balance between pestering the news media about mundane things and ignoring the value of important news. Individual schools often think in terms of the human interest story associated with particular school events.

These are particularly appropriate for community newspapers, whose readers are likely to be parents or relatives of your students. But the public is also interested in curriculum and special programs (how and what the students are learning).

Who Gets the Word Out

Appoint a media coordinator or contact person. He or she will soon become knowledgeable about where to send news releases and how to get news on the radio or television. Don't discourage any staff members

---

The following additional ideas are reprinted from the Principals' Survival Packet published by NSPRA.

It started in Palo Alto, Calif., where a group of parents got together and developed guidelines to "help parents try to keep their youngsters free of drugs and alcohol, away from unsupervised parties and aware of reasonable limits." It was called "Parents Who Care." Parents in Green Bay, Wis., picked up the Calif. idea and with a few changes, the program became "Families Who Care."

The guidelines are divided into four main sections by each group. Here is what they developed. With local changes they could be adapted by any school group.

Family communication is vital: Know where to reach each other by phone. Be aware or be awakened, when your children come home at night. Assure your children they can telephone you to be picked up whenever needed. Get to know your children's friends and their parents. Support all school regulations as a family.

Reasonable hours are necessary for safety and a sense of security: On school nights, children should be home unless employed or attending school, church, or community events, in which cases they should come home a half hour after the activity ends. On weekend eve-

from drumming up their own publicity for special projects. Sometimes when the person directly involved with the story—the faculty advisor or the program director—makes the contact, his or her enthusiasm awakens immediate interest and gains coverage when someone farther removed from the event cannot.

Consider whether parents might know (or be) someone who can get your story to the media. Explore, develop and exploit your local resources. And, by all means, send a copy of your announcement to the school district's public relations office, to the superintendent, and board of education members.

Preparing a News Release

As a common means of disseminating information, the news release is just as suitable to the individual school as to the district or regional agency. Some general principles apply to all news releases:

nings, the guidelines suggest sixth graders and under stay home except for the activities mentioned above; 7th and 8th graders be home from 9:30 to 10:00; 9th and 10th graders 10:30 to 11:00; 11th graders 11:30 to 12:00; and 12th graders 12:30.

Social life: As a parent you are legally responsible for minor children and their actions. Be alert to signs of drug and alcohol abuse, and be aware that driving after drinking or drug use is a crime. When a child is going to a party, feel free to contact host parents to verify the occasion and check on supervision, and ask them what will,

and will not, be served. As a host parent, encourage your children to tell their friends that their parents are welcome to inquire about the party. Encourage small parties, ask anyone with drugs or alcohol to leave—and not come back—and be a visible host or hostess. Unoccupied homes are frequent party sites, so provide for house supervision when you are away.

Malls and/or shopping centers: Be sure your children know where to go for help if problems occur. Encourage reasonable time limits for shopping. And be aware of the amount of money your children have to spend and what items are brought home.

☐ Make them easy to read, easy to edit, easy to verify.

☐ A preprinted masthead saves you time and gives a professional appearance.

☐ Type the release double- or triple-spaced on one side only of 8" × 11" paper.

☐ Restrict copy to a single page, if possible.

☐ Mention opportunities for photographs in the release or include good quality black and white glossy photos. Identification of pictures should be on a separate sheet of paper pasted to the back of the picture, not written directly on the photograph.

☐ Allow 10 days to two weeks lead time.

☐ Hand deliver, if possible. If sent through the mail, direct them to a specific person whom you have identified in advance as the best contact.

NAME OF SCHOOL   DATE

ADDRESS OF SCHOOL

CONTACT PERSON AND TITLE

PHONE NUMBER: (Home and School)

COPY: Begin one-third down the page

LEAD: First paragraph should include who, what, where, when, why and how.

BODY: Include further details. Plan to get your most important facts in the first few lines, with information in decreasing order of importance to the end. If space is tight, stories are cut from the bottom up.

Give facts, not opinions.

Show the end # # #
Or "More"

Many building principals are finding the weekly mailing of a **Media Tip Sheet** the answer to their school coverage. Pulling together four or five (or more) story ideas that the media might be interested in covering, they prepare brief paragraphs with a head to attract attention, give the "who, what, when, where and how," and most importantly the name of the person to be contacted for more detail and the phone number to call (home and school). Media response is most favorable according to those using this technique.

Schools and the Non-Native Population

As more and more communities experience influxes of foreign-born families, the schools are rising to new challenges. Teachers and administrators must be especially sensitive to the potential pitfalls in trying to

Bridging the Cultural Gap

Betty Knight, director of the English for Speakers of Other Languages/Bilingual Program for the Montgomery County (Md.) Public Schools, provides these suggestions:

1. Never take for granted that just because a person seems fluent in English that he or she really understands everything you're saying. Speak slowly. Voice inflection is an integral part of verbal communication in many cultures, so failing to keep your voice calm and level will add to the confusion.

2. Watch your non-verbal communication even more. Each society has its own rules of "acceptable" behavior—standards for being polite and gracious. For example:
   □ Mexicans consider closeness and touching a demonstration of friendship, while people from most Asian countries find that kind of behavior offensive.
   □ Summoning a Filipino with the traditional American gesture of curling the fingers inward with the palm up is degrading.
   □ Thumbs-up sign meaning "okay" to us is an ob-

scene gesture to a Brazilian.
□ One country's goodbye wave is another's "come here" sign.
□ Showing an Arab the sole of your shoe as you cross your legs is an insult.
□ The teacher who complains about the little girl who won't look at her when she is being reprimanded doesn't understand that Hispanics, and Koreans, too, are taught that eyes down is a mark of respect to a teacher.
□ Japanese culture requires an evenness of mood and expression and Japanese people are taught never to show emotion. This can be very frustrating to a teacher who tries harder and harder to get the new child "excited" about the class project—but think of what it does to the child!

communicate with someone from another country—whether in working with the children in the classroom or dealing with parents at a conference.

Every school district with a sizable non-native population should provide guidance for its staff to alert them to the do's and don'ts of dealing with people from other cultures. Remember to send out school information, newsletters and/or invitations in the other language(s) used by your school parents and have a person call who can speak the language. Be sure to have bilingual people at all meetings and on duty in the school office, so that parents and students (until they learn to communicate in English) can express themselves in the language they speak and know that you will listen to what they say.

Schedule language courses for students, parents, and members of the non-native population in the community. Show them that the school cares.

Student Community Service

Another sure-fire PR plus is involving students in community service projects.

Students of the Sun View Elementary School in Ocean View, Calif., held a Community Health Fair at the school, where, through the cooperation of school district nurses and community health organizations, a wide range of medical tests was made available to the public.

During the fair, sixth graders put on a puppet show on good health habits, still another facet to overwhelming community acceptance.

At the McCluer High School in the Ferguson-Florissant (Mo.) School District, seniors, instead of making the traditional class gift to their school, pledged a gift of service to their community. They went out and helped needy families, provided transportation for senior citizens, and did house and yard work in the community.

Thousands of school children have joined hands with community groups across the nation to raise money for restoring the Statue of Liberty and for the African relief fund.

Home Visits

When parents won't or can't come to the school, the school can go to the parents.

Invariably, in school districts throughout the country, when teachers visit the home to help parents help their children, several things happen:

□ Parents are impressed. They get more involved, especially in coming to future parent/teacher conferences. They see teachers in a new, more positive light.

□ The teachers get a far better understanding of the pupil and his or her parents and home life, helping the teacher to better serve the child.

□ The lower achieving student's performance in class usually improves.

Again, however, a project like this must be a voluntary, cooperative effort involving the principal, the teacher and the parent. Mandates won't work.

Visits to homes are particularly effective for families new to the community. A good new-family orientation program should be somewhat like the one set up by the Norris Elementary School in Omaha, Neb. As part of the program:

□ A guidance counselor or parent volunteer visits new families that move into the area during the summer and throughout the year.

□ The principal visits new families during the summer months.

□ New students are introduced to other neighborhood children and given a tour of the school.

□ Printed information about the school is provided for new families.

□ A new-family orientation meeting is scheduled at the school at the beginning of the school year.

□ New families receive special invitations from the principal to attend various school events.

School Meals

Many schools feel that the way to a community's heart is through its stomach. They use breakfasts and lunches to bring people into the school.

At the Greenbriar West Elementary School in Fairfax, Va., the project is called "Dime-a-Dip." Families are invited to come and bring a covered dish that will feed six persons. Food donations are coordinated so there will be a wide variety. The event is advertised in the school paper, the local paper and by memos to parents, with a tearoff return slip at the bottom of each notice.

On the night of the dinner, participants pay a dime for each dip of food they take, providing a family of four with a meal for about $2.50.

It's a big event and requires much planning, an active PTA and a lot of parental volunteers, but it is extremely popular with the community and its fosters increased community participation in other school activities.

Senior Citizens

Schools also will find a ready group of communicators in senior citizens. If senior citizens are involved in school activities they will be among its most active boosters.

The most common service given senior citizens by schools is the "Golden Age Card," which admits them free to school district activities like plays, musical presentations and sporting events. But there are many more ways to cater to the senior citizens, such as Grandparents Day or a visitors center in the school where they can chat with school staff informally. Children take visitors on school tours to let them observe classes and teachers, and hand out information sheets explaining classroom activities.

Many schools are launching extensive programs to both involve and serve the growing numbers of senior citizens in their communities; many of whom are still extremely active and interested in working with students. Such programs include serving hot meals, recruiting seniors to tutor students, share their talents, and work as volunteers in the school office and library. Intergenerational programs in music, art, drama and in actual classroom instruction are growing.

Empty classrooms are being turned into community day care centers in many areas providing facilities not only for programs for pre-school children, but for senior citizens needing care. The opportunities are vast and PR conscious principals are working with their community groups to identify the needs of this critical group of non-parents and provide ways to involve and serve them.

Appreciation Day

Based on the theory that nothing improves a person's morale more than praise, Appreciation Day can be publicized as the time to say a special thank-you to: teachers, custodians, cafeteria workers, school board, bus drivers, clericals, central office, parent volunteers, students, crossing guards, etc.

Everyone can become involved. For ideas to help you develop an Appreciation Day for your school, here are some ways people from the North Allegheny (Pa.) Public Schools found to say "Thanks, you're appreciated."

□ Notes to each different employee group from the superintendent.

□ Packs of Lifesavers to the instructional and media aides.

□ A note to each clerical staff member—saying, "You Deserve a Break," with a packet of coffee enclosed.

□ A potholder, from a curriculum coordinator to those who gave a helping hand, when a helping hand was needed.

☐ Notes of appreciation to school board members.

☐ Flowers to secretaries.

☐ Donuts and coffee for staff, compliments of the building principal.

☐ Personalized letters to students recognizing special accomplishments.

☐ A cookout for maintenance workers.

☐ Fruit baskets.

☐ Student-sponsored "clean-up" day to say thanks to custodians.

☐ Personal phone calls to and from staff; to and from parents.

☐ Telegrams saying thanks.

☐ Special recognition assemblies for staff, students, parent and community volunteers.

☐ Invitations to senior citizens to share in "We Appreciate You" activities.

☐ Invitations to community leaders, legislators, clergy, etc., inviting them to a special luncheon, or program to show—"We Appreciate You."

☐ Letters to school vendors and others who serve the schools to say thank you.

Appreciation Days are becoming a vital part of most school district and building programs. The National Parent Teachers Association has identified the first week of May as Teacher Appreciation Week.

CHAPTER FOURTEEN

Evaluating Your PR Investment

Two systematic approaches to evaluation in public relations are communication audits and evaluation of PR objectives. The audit evaluation system is a good place to start when the results can be used in planning new strategies and activities to achieve the overall goals of a school system.

Evaluating PR objectives is a natural follow-up to the audit as new, measurable objectives are usually generated from it. In both cases, top management must be committed to acting on recommendations or the lengthy evaluation process will become a frustrating game played by a select few and most likely enjoyed by none.

Communication Audits

A communication audit is an analysis of your school district's communications—internal and external. It is designed to take a snapshot of your system's communication needs, policies, activities, capabilities and programs. It involves staff and community leaders and leads to a set of recommendations from a communication expert to be acted upon by your administrative cabinet and school board.

A comprehensive audit will uncover communication gaps and suggest:
- Short- and long-term goals
- Priority of those goals
- Themes/issues to be emphasized
- Priority list of publics
- Community pulse on key issues
- Communication methods that are working
- New communication methods warranted
- A measuring stick for future evaluation.

The audit is perhaps the best method to evaluate a long-term program in school PR. It pinpoints strengths and weaknesses, uncovers needs and usually gives validity for doing more in school PR.

Topics Audits Cover

Major topics covered in school district audits include:

□ Communication philosophy: review of formal policies, management's openness, management's support of communication, role of PR office, centralized versus decentralized approach, etc.

□ Community demographics: analysis of who is there now and who may be there in five years, activity or stability of the community, private school students, percentage of non-parents, etc.

□ Objectives and goals of school district and PR office.

□ Organization and staffing of PR office.

□ Existing PR program: review of products, activities and general program for internal and external public relations.

□ Attitudes toward present PR program: internal and external publics report on current program—its strengths and weaknesses.

□ Needs and expectations: feedback from all consulted groups.

Five Basic Steps

A school district communication audit follows five basic steps:

1. Researching—reviewing current program and data on school and community.
2. Finding out what "we" think: talking to key management and assessing the school district's strengths and weaknesses in instruction, management and public relations.
3. Finding out what "they" think: going to key internal and external publics and seeking their opinions on strengths and weaknesses in instruction, management and public relations.
4. Evaluating the difference between what "we" and "they" said: developing a PR balance sheet of assets, liabilities, strengths and weaknesses.
5. Recommending how to close the gaps uncovered in the audit.

More information on actually completing an audit is available from the National School Public Relations Association.

Audits often create a new perspective on public relations among school administrators and employees. They see the need for a systematic approach to school PR and realize that publicity and one-shot activities do not constitute a PR program. The results of audits usually lead to new PR plans, strategies and objectives which, when drafted correctly, can assist in the annual evaluation of your PR program.

Evaluating PR Objectives

Much of what school PR programs do is measurable. To deny that a large portion of PR deals with human relations, courtesy, goodwill and persuading people to like and support our schools would be wrong. But most PR activities produce results that are measurable and that can help prove the worth of your PR program.

The evaluation of PR objectives is defined by Nager and Allen in *Public Relations: Management by Objectives* as a total management system that focuses on results rather than on activities for performance evaluation. They also ask us to consider the following questions about the practice of PR:

1. Why is public relations vital to your organization's management?
2. What does public relations do for the organization?
3. How are public relations priorities set?
4. How is the public relations department evaluated?
5. How effectively are public relations resources utilized?
6. To what results can the public relations department point?
7. How does the public relations department support and contribute to the organization's goals?

The PR objective approach to evaluation allows you to tie your objectives into your school district goals. It also permits you to focus on those areas where you feel measurable results will do your program and school district the most good.

The evaluation of PR objectives must become part of the office's routine or it may not be worth the extra effort. Ways are often found to insert some evaluative questions into feedback devices already planned for *regular* programs throughout the year.

Some PR people view evaluating objectives as just a "numbers-for-numbers-sake" game, but if used effectively, it can enhance the credibility and management status of the PR program. The advice from PR specialists using PR objectives in evaluation is to move as much as you can toward measurable objectives. Your first attempts at PR objective evaluation will be far from perfect, but as you move toward measurability, you will gain the respect of your colleagues because you are charting a path as to why an investment in PR is a sound strategy for your school system.

Using Focus Groups

Focus groups are often used in a communication audit. They must be carefully selected so that they are representative of the groups you wish to reach. A listing of possible focus groups for a school district audit are:

1. Superintendent and key central office managers.
2. Board president and board members.
3. Middle management—principals/assistant principals/supervisors.
4. Teachers/counselors/nurses.

5. Secretaries/custodians/aides/bus drivers.
6. Parent group leaders.
7. Non-parent representatives.
8. Media representatives.
9. High school seniors.
10. Government leaders/business officers.

The Focus Sessions

Groups of seven to 12 people work best in focus groups. Members are selected and then invited by a school official to attend a 45- to 90-minute meeting to share their opinions on the purpose of the audit—to improve communications.

No other information is actually needed by participants because the auditors are seeking their opinion on specific questions to be asked of all members at the group session. Notes are taken by the auditors but no attribution is ever assigned to an individual. Taping the sessions is also discouraged.

The results of the focus groups interviews are then used to build a survey for further, scientific feedback or used as indication of what these groups are thinking in the auditor's final report. If you are after representative feedback that can be scientifically scrutinized, you need to implement a formal random survey discussed elsewhere in this book. If you are after an indication of what these groups are feeling and thinking, the focus group techniques should suffice.

Take Action if Needed

A good superintendent, board member, principal or PR person knows, instinctively, whether or not true communication is taking place, or if a school district or a school board or a school itself is just going through the motions.

If, deep down, you know something is wrong, then do something about it! And the first thing you might do is answer the following questions:

1. Does the district have a written, clear and concise policy statement regarding its public relations program?
2. Is the policy statement approved by the school board, published in its policy manual and reviewed annually?
3. Does the policy statement express the purposes of the public relations program and provide for the delegation of such authority as necessary to achieve the purposes to an appropriate administrator?
4. Is the policy statement included in the district personnel handbook so that all staff members are aware of the purposes of the public relations program?

5. Is the public relations program allocated sufficient human and financial resources to accomplish its goals?
6. Is the public relations program part of the management function and does the person directing these efforts have the necessary skills and training to do the job?
7. Is the public relations officer/director directly responsible to the superintendent?
8. Does the public relations unit or officer have the authority to initiate or suggest such research studies as are necessary to carry out the objectives of the program?
9. Does the program provide for effective means of internal communication?
10. Does the public relations unit utilize feedback continuously to modify its activities to meet the information needs of its audiences?
11. Does the public relations program conduct inservice training for other members of the school staff in the area of school/community relations?
12. Does the public relations program have procedures for identifying specific individuals and groups with whom continuous communication and relationships are necessary?
13. Are there procedures for determining what kinds of information should be supplied, with particular emphasis on relative importance and the degree of public interest?
14. Does the program use a variety of appropriate communication media channels to get the message across?
15. Does the program encourage, receive, analyze and utilize feedback on its activities?
16. Does the program encourage community involvement in the schools?
17. Is there provision for continuous and systematic evaluation?

Answers to the above will tell you almost conclusively if you have the proper climate, organization and implementation of a good, professional school public relations program.

Of course, the questions above are just a beginning. Each district must formulate its own detailed set of evaluation criteria for its individual programs.

They will not, however, tell you if you are succeeding. Only your publics can tell you that. But if you don't listen, you'll never know. And when you finally hear, it will be too late.

Conclusion

School public relations is more than a phrase, more than a project or a program, more than a budgeted activity. Far more.

It is a climate, a commitment, a mission, a passion—if you will—to build public confidence in education.

Public relations is more than just words. It is action; planned, continuous action, day-by-day, month-by-month, year-by-year, to convince the public of this country through communication and quality education that the public schools are, indeed, the backbone of our nation's commitment to democracy, and, as such, they must be preserved, supported and improved.

The commitment to action must be an all-consuming one. It must start with the board of education, where the policy, the climate, the tone of the school district is set. It must emanate strongly from the superintendent and it must filter down through the ranks to the classroom aide and the school crossing guard.

It is a task for the entire school family, not just the public relations person or the board president or the superintendent of schools.

This book is a resource book of ideas, a catalogue of tools, a dictionary of resources to be applied to the effort to strengthen public confidence and support of education today.

Its contents prove conclusively that the job can be and is being done in schools and school districts throughout the country.

It traces the rise of the enterprise of American education in the face of the Commission of Excellence critique. Its reaction was, in the most part, exemplary. In a rare, united effort, it admitted its weaknesses and pledged to improve them, while at the same time showcasing its historic strengths and accomplishments as well as its future goals and aspirations.

But a one-time, counter-attack, finger-in-the-dike approach to educational public relations is not enough. Far from it. A continuing, pervasive, all-encompassing national communications effort is critically necessary if education is to take advantage of the window of opportunity in which it finds itself in the sunset of the 1980s.

Education is at the top of the nation's agenda. It is centered in the fishbowl of public scrutiny. It is an enterprise perched at the peak of public interest, pausing momentarily, precariously, either before solidifying its position as the bedrock of our national way of life or sliding backward toward uncertainty, doubt and an eroding base of public support.

Historically, as the pendulum swings, can its forward momentum be maintained?

The answer is yes, it can.

But *will* it be maintained?

The answer is up to us.

NATIONAL SCHOOL PUBLIC RELATIONS ASSOCIATION

Code of Ethics

The educational public relations professional shall:

I. Be guided constantly by pursuit of the public interest through truth, accuracy, good taste, and fairness—
   - following good judgment in releasing information
   - not intentionally disseminating misinformation or confidential data
   - avoiding actions which lessen personal, professional or organizational reputation.

II. Give primary loyalty to the employing organization, insisting on the right to give advisory counsel in accordance with sound public relations ideas and practices—
   - cooperating with other groups while avoiding conflicts with primary responsibilities
   - objecting to untenable or unethical policies and activities.

III. Be aware of personal influence, avoiding promises or granting of unprofessional advantages to others—
   - refraining from accepting special considerations for influence on organizational decisions
   - refraining from unauthorized use of organizational facilities, resources or professional services for personal gain or for promotion of the candidacy of aspirants for elected offices.

IV. Recognize that effectiveness is dependent upon integrity and regard for ideas of the profession—
   - not misrepresenting professional qualifications
   - giving credit for ideas and words borrowed from others
   - cooperating with professional colleagues to uphold and enforce this Code.

NATIONAL SCHOOL PUBLIC RELATIONS ASSOCIATION

Standards for Educational Public Relations Programs

Educational public relations is a planned and systematic management function to help improve the programs and services of an educational organization. It relies on a comprehensive two-way communications process involving both internal and external publics, with a goal of stimulating a better understanding of the role, objectives, accomplishments, and needs of the organization. Educational public relations programs assist in interpreting public attitudes, identify and help shape policies and procedures in the public interest, and carry on involvement and information activities which earn public understanding and support.

I. Concept
  A. Policy
    1. The organization shall adopt a clear and concise public relations policy statement.
    2. The policy statement shall be approved through formal action of the organization's governing body, shall be published in its policy manual, and shall be reviewed annually by the governing body.
    3. The policy statement shall express the purposes of the organization's public relations program and shall provide for the delegation of authority to appropriate executives.
  B. Procedures
    1. Management shall clarify the public relations policies through the development of written operational procedures.
    2. The procedures shall outline major components of the public relations programs, detail rules and regulations, and specify employee roles and responsibilities.

3. The procedures shall be distributed to all employees and representatives of key external publics.

II. Resources

Commitment to the achievement of the purposes of the organization's public relations policy shall be demonstrated through the allocation of adequate human and financial resources to the public relations program.

A. Staff
   1. The staffing of a public relations program will vary according to an organization's size, needs, and availability of resources. In every situation, however, the responsibility shall be assigned to an individual who reports directly to the chief executive officer and who participates as a full member of the administrative cabinet.
   2. Recognition of public relations as a management function of primary importance shall be demonstrated through the existence of a unit staffed by full-time professional public relations personnel. Staff size shall be sufficient to accomplish the objectives of the organization and to cope with the variety of inherent conditions and problems.
   3. The public relations staff shall meet NSPRA's Standards for Educational Public Relations Professionals.
   4. Provision shall be made for continuous training and development for members of the public relations staff.

B. Budget
   1. The organization's budget shall include a specific item for public relations staffing, services, and programs.
   2. The amount of the public relations budget will vary according to organizational needs. However, in addition to staff, appropriate provisions shall be made for the following: materials and equipment; facilities; technical services (publications, advertising, audiovisual, radio, television, etc.); involvement activities; professional growth and development; research and evaluation.
   3. Provisions shall be made for appropriate public relations activities in the budgets of each of the organization's major departments and programs.

III. Internal Communications

The basic foundation of the organization's public relations program shall be a sound and effective system of internal communications.

A. Planning
1. The organization shall develop a written plan which identifies key internal audiences, as well as procedures for determining the kind of information they need and desire.
2. Each major department, program, or unit in the organization shall develop appropriate communications strategies based on the overall plan.

B. Implementation
1. An appropriate variety of communications methods shall be used, including vehicles for encouraging, receiving, analyzing, and using feedback.
2. A continuing public relations training program shall be provided for the entire staff or membership of the organization.

IV. External Communications
The organization shall be committed to ongoing, creative efforts to inform and involve external publics.

A. Planning
1. The organization shall develop a written plan which identifies key community individuals and groups, as well as procedures for determining the kind of information they need and desire.
2. Each major department, program or unit in the organization will develop appropriate communications strategies based on the overall plan.

B. Implementation
1. An appropriate variety of communications methods shall be used.
2. Special efforts shall be made to encourage, receive, analyze, and use feedback.
3. Strategies shall be developed to identify and involve community resources.

V. Accountability
A. Program Performance
1. The organization shall provide for evaluation of the public relations program based on proposed objectives and the degree to which they have been achieved.
2. The staff or membership of the organization shall be included in any evaluation process.

B. Development
1. The organization shall provide for long-range public relations planning.

2. The organization shall develop a plan for anticipating, preparing for, and dealing with the public relations aspects of unusual or crisis situations.

3. Emphasis shall be given to seeking and developing new and different avenues of communications and relationships.

NATIONAL SCHOOL PUBLIC RELATIONS ASSOCIATION

Standards for Educational Public Relations Professionals

An educational public relations professional is a person who performs public relations functions in a staff or executive capacity with an eductional organization.

I. General Standards
   General standards for an educational public relations professional shall include:
   A. Understanding and acceptance of the role of education in a free society.
   B. Understanding and acceptance of the role and social responsibility of public relations for all educational institutions, organizations, and agencies in a free society.
   C. Commitment to the improvement of educational opportunity for all.
   D. Professional performance and ethical behavior in educational public relations as described in NSPRA's Ethics for Educational Public Relations.

II. Specific Standards
   A. Professional Preparation
      1. Minimum of a Bachelor's Degree from an accredited college or university.
      2. Study in the area of public relations, behavioral sciences, management, and education.

B. Experience

Standards for experience shall include at least one of the following:

1. Two years' full-time experience in an executive public relations responsibility with an educational organization.

2. Three years' full-time experience (or the equivalent time) in a staff public relations responsibility with an educational organization.

3. Three years' full-time experience in an executive public relations responsibility with an organization outside the area of education, plus one year in a professional capacity with an educational organization.

4. Four years' full-time experience in a staff public relations responsibility with an organization outside the area of education plus one year in a professional capacity with an educational organization.

5. Four years' full-time experience in mass communications (press, radio, television, etc.) with news, editorial or program responsibilities, plus one year in a professional capacity with an educational organization.

6. Five years' full-time experience in a professional capacity with an educational organization, plus one year in a full-time public relations responsibility.

7. Three years' full-time experience as a college teacher of school public relations or related communications courses, plus one year in a full-time public relations responsibility with an educational organization or three years of significant public relations consultant experience to educational organizations.

C. Demonstrated Ability

Standards for demonstrated ability shall include, in general, a working knowledge of comprehensive internal and external public relations programs, a mastery of basic communications skills, and a sensitivity to the importance of two-way communication.

Specifically, the educational public relations professional shall demonstrate these abilities through the following:

1. Employing effective human relations practices in the performance of public relations responsibilities.

2. Perceiving, identifying, and determining the implications of educational public relations problems.

3. Creating, proposing, and conducting activities designed to solve educational public relations problems

4. Conducting continuous public relations activities that depend on the nature, structure, and functions of mass media.

5. Planning, developing, and executing specific public relations projects essential to campaigns, interpretation of innovations, or other major activities.

6. Planning, developing, and using feedback processes, including opinion surveys.

7. Identifying and working with elements of power structures.

8. Identifying and working with individuals and citizens groups in the development and execution of the organization's program.

9. Involving staff and/or members of the organization in the development and execution of the organization's public relations program.

D. Professional Growth and Development

Standards for professional growth and development require that educational public relations professionals continue to refine skills and expand knowledge through:

1. Maintaining membership and participation in NSPRA and other professional public relations associations and societies.

2. Participating in the NSPRA National Seminar and other recognized public relations seminars, conferences, workshops, and institutes.

3. Pursuing additional study beyond Bachelor's Degree requirements in pertinent areas.

4. Reading, researching, writing, speaking, and consulting in public relations.

5. Seeking NSPRA accreditation.

Policy

Public Information Program
Tacoma, Washington Public Schools

The Board of Directors of Tacoma School District No. 10 believes it is the responsibility of each Board member, as well as each employee of the District, to actively pursue a two-day communications program that highlights the educational experiences in the city's public schools and promotes effective school/home/community partnerships.

The Board recognizes that citizens have a right to know what is occurring in their public school system; that Board members and all school administrators have an obligation to see that all publics are kept systematically and adequately informed; and that the District will benefit from seeing that citizens get all information, good and bad, directly from the system itself.

The Board affirms the following objectives:

1. To maintain an effective two-way communication system between the District and its various publics which ensures:
   a) Dissemination of accurate, timely information about school policies, programs, procedures, achievements, decisions, critical issues;
   b) Interpretation of decisions and action;
   c) Elimination of rumors and misinformation;
   d) Programs and practices designed to provide an open climate which will elicit ideas, suggestions, reactions from the community and employees alike;
   e) An effective working relationship with the news media.
2. To maintain a Public Information Office which will coordinate the District's effective and other communities.
3. To develop and maintain an organizational environment where all District staff members are aware that they share the responsibility for communication of school policies, programs and activities to parents, members of the educational and other communities.

4. To maintain a written plan of communication policies and guidelines which will be available to employees and to the public upon request.
5. To support the establishment of a Communications Review Committee to review and evaluate Districtwide two-way communication efforts.

"The Board of Directors of any school district shall have authority to authorize the expenditure of funds for the purpose of preparing and distributing information to the general public to explain the instructional program, operation and maintenance of the schools of the district: Provided, that nothing contained herein shall be construed to authorize preparation and distribution of information to the general public for the purpose of influencing the outcome of a school district election."

Board members believe it is essential to the development of excellence in the education of Tacoma youngsters that the maximum possible knowledge about the goals, achievements, activities and operations of the school district be conveyed to the students, staff and citizens.

The Board therefore reaffirms its commitment to openness in relationships with its patrons as states in Policy 1110. The Board further believes that the citizens of Tacoma, as well as the staff and students, should be consulted and involved in the problem-solving and decision-making processes at as early a stage as possible. This involvement should be solicited actively and honestly through a wide variety of means.

Source: Tacoma (Wash.) Public Schools.

Job Description

Director of Communication

Westside Community Schools, District 66, Omaha, Neb.

Position: Director of Communications

To Whom Responsible: Superintendent

For Whom Responsible: Communications Department, administrators and staff members as superintendent's assignments designate

Main Function: To direct internal and external school-community relations programs for the school system

Responsibilities:

Administration

☐ To administer districtwide functions as designated by the superintendent

☐ To develop and direct a planned, systematic program of communications

☐ To direct the district's communications program on a local, state and national basis, with major emphasis on communications within the district, communications between the student's school and home, and communications between the district and the community

☐ To serve as a communications liaison between the press and the superintendent and staff members

☐ To be knowledgeable of all major happenings within the district as a basis for accurate reporting and communicating

☐ To arrange for press coverage at all major functions of the district

☐ To organize and plan regular meetings for communication advisory group, made up of community leaders

☐ To maintain a working relationship with community leaders and community organizations, such as the Chamber of Commerce

☐ To serve as an advisor to the superintendent and as a member of the superintendent's administrative council

☐ To represent the school system in community, state and national functions, as requested by the superintendent.

Personnel

☐ To work with administrators, staff members and community volunteers in planning and developing public relations programs and strategies for both one-way and two-way communications

☐ To plan, develop and maintain channels for communication with all staff.

Curriculum

☐ To be well informed about the school programs, and activities as a basis for communication needs

☐ To serve as a communications consultant for various district curriculum committees

☐ To develop communication plans for curriculum adoptions.

Staff Development

☐ To work with the director of staff development in developing and leading communication workshops for staff members, as needed and requested

☐ To provide staff development programs for the communications staff.

Communications

☐ To manage the operation of the communication department with direct responsibility for department personnel, budget development, materials and equipment

☐ To manage the development and production of district publications for staff and community

☐ To direct the functions of the printing office for administrative, curriculum, and communication purposes

☐ To develop and maintain an effective working relationship with the news media

☐ To prepare news releases, organize news conferences and prepare informational programs

☐ To assist any staff member or group of employees to tell a story of what's happening educationally, by news story, slide presentation, speech, article, media announcement

☐ To be a consultant in organizing and conducting effective meetings and conferences.

Finance

☐ To annually submit proposed budgetary items for the communications department to the superintendent

☐ To be accountable for all approved budgetary expenditures allocated to the communications department.

The Nation's Education Flag

The Flag of Learning and Liberty

Flag of Learning and Liberty
National School Public Relations Association

On July 4, 1985, the first flag symbolizing the link between education and a strong, free nation was raised over the capitals of all 50 states and the District of Columbia.

The *Flag of Learning and Liberty* was inspired by recent national attention on the importance of education and significant reform movements undertaken by many states.

American education, learning and liberty, has its roots in the founding of America. The leaders of the American Revolution saw education as a means of preserving liberty, securing unity, promoting good citizenship and developing resources of the land and people. They believed education would help maintain the union of states, a united people and a democratic form of government.

On the occasion of the 50th anniversary of the National School Public Relations Association (NSPRA) in 1985, several thousand prominent citizens were asked to contribute their ideas about education and how it might be improved. Their statements, reflecting the same deep commitment to education found in the words of our forefathers, were used as the basis for the flag's design. The effort was made possible through the assistance of The Southland Corporation.

The *Flag of Learning and Liberty* incorporates the red, white and blue of the "Stars and Stripes," and symbolizes America's historical belief in and reliance upon education.

The nation's education flag features:

□ *A horizontal red strip* across its top depicting the strength and vitality of a democratic way of life.

□ *A blue strip* running horizontally along the bottom which represents the stability and opportunity made possible by a strong system of education.

□ *A center field of white* which conveys the virtue and aspiration of a nation of free people.

The central focus of the flag is the emblem in the middle of the field. The design features:

□ *Two gold flames* at the top—one for learning and one for liberty. These flames are supported by a base of four elements, arranged in alternating blue and red pairs.

□ The *blue elements* represent the two key foundations of strong education—high expectations and effective teaching.

□ The *red elements* symbolize the cornerstone institutins of a democratic society—responsible families and involved communities.

Educators must continue their efforts to help the public understand the importance of education in our democratic society.

We can now fly the *Flag of Learning and Liberty* in every classroom, over every school building, public and private, every school district and every public institution in America. The symbol will serve as a constant reminder to focus the public's attention upon the critical role education plays in our democratic society. (For additional information about the *Flag of Learning and Liberty,* contact NSPRA.)

References

Bernays, Edward L. *Crystallizing Public Opinion.* Boni and Liveright, 1961.

Bernays, Edward L. *The Engineering of Consent.* University of Oklahoma Press, 1956.

Cutlip, Scott M., and Allen A. Center. *Effective Public Relations.* 5th ed. Prentice-Hall, 1982.

Grunig, James E., and Todd Hunt. *Managing Public Relations.* Holt, Rinehart and Winston, 1984.

Kindred, Leslie W., Don Bagin, and Don Gallagher. *The School and Community Relations.* 3rd ed. Prentice-Hall, 1984.

Drucker, Peter F. *Management: Tasks, Practices, Responsibilities.* Harper and Row, 1974.

Drucker, Peter F. *The Changing World of the Executive.* Truman Talley Books. 1982.

Oveal, W. *Theory Z: How American Business Can Meet the Japanese Challenge.* Avon, 1982.

Peters and Austin. *A Passion for Excellence.* Random House, 1985.

Peters and Waterman. *In Search of Excellence.* Harper and Row, 1982.

Chase, W. Howard. *Issue Management: Origins of the Future.* Issue Action Publications, 1984.

Neill, Shirley Boes, ed. *Planning for Tomorrow's Schools: Problems and Solutions. AASA Critical Issues Report.* American Association of School Administrators, 1983.

Issues Management Newsletter, published every other month by Issue Management Association, Washington, D.C.

John Naisbitt Trendletter, published twice a month by Naisbitt Group, Washington, D.C.

Finn, David. *Public Relations and Management.* Reinhold, 1980.

"Ten-Step Communication Planner." Bob Grossman, Los Angeles County Office of Education, 1983.

Public Relations for Administrators, American Association of School Administrators, 1985.

Strunk, William, and E. B. White. *The Elements of Style.* Macmillan, 1972.

Jones, Clarence. *How to Speak T.V.* Kukar and Co., Inc., 1983.

Banach, William J., and Ernest L. Stech. *The Banach-Stech Communication Audit,* 1981.

School PR-Everybody's Job, National Association of Secondary School Principals, 1981.

"How to Start and Improve a PR Program, Don Bagin, National School Boards Association, 1975.

PR For School Board Members, American Association of School Administrators, 1976.

Radio: Your Publics are Listening, National School Boards Association, 1976.

Without Bias: A Guidebook for Nondiscriminatory Communication, International Association of Business Communicators, 1977.

From NSPRA

Choices in Schools: What's Ahead and What To Do?, 1985.
Learn From the Winners: School PR Programs That Work, 1983.
Good Schools: What Makes Them Work, 1981.
Good Teachers: What To Look For, 1981.
The Nation's Report Card, 1985, 1985.
Building-Level PR Programs, 1980.
Building Public Confidence for Your Schools, 1978.
Evaluating Your School PR Investment, 1984.
Survey/Feedback, 1980.
Working With The Media, 1980.
New Voices on the Right: Impact on Schools, 1982.
Basic School Public Relations Kit, 1980.
Involving All Your Publics, 1980.
Keys to Community Involvement, 1984.
School Communication Workshop Kit, 1979.
You Can Win at the Polls: A Finance Campaign Kit, 1980.
PR Programs for Small, Suburban, and Large Districts, 1980.
School Labor Strife: Rebuilding the Team, 1982.
Principals' Survival Packets, Volumes I & II, 1983.
Publications for Effective Communications, 1980.
Board Member/Superintendent PR Survival Packet, 1985.
Lighting the Fire: A Process for Building Staff Morale and Excellence, 1984.
Non-Parents and Schools: Creating a New Team, 1982.
Staff Recognition: Unlocking the Potential for Success, 1985.
101 PR Ideas You Can Use Now . . . And More!, 1986.
RALLY SCHOOL SUPPORT: Your Campaign To Build Commitment For Education In A Democratic Society, 1986.

Periodicals

Education USA, National School Public Relations Assn.
IT STARTS in the Classroom, National School Public Relations Assn.
ED-LINE—National School Public Relations Assn., Education's Electronic
  Communication Network
communication briefings, 806 Westminster Blvd., Blackwood, N.J. 08012
PR News, 127 East 80th Street, New York, N.Y. 10021
pr reporter, PO Box 600, Exeter, N.H. 03833
NSPRA Network, National School Public Relations Assn.
Communication World, International Assn. of Business Communicators, 870
  Market St., Suite 940, San Francisco, CA 94102
Public Relations Journal, Public Relations Society of America, 845 Third Avenue,
  New York, N.Y. 10022
NSPRA IMPACT, Journal of the National School Public Relations Assn.
Scanner, National School Public Relations Assn.

Index